I0415697

January 2012

DODD-FRANK ACT

Hybrid Capital Instruments and Small Institution Access to Capital

GAO
Accountability * Integrity * Reliability

January 2012

DODD-FRANK ACT

Hybrid Capital Instruments and Small Institution Access to Capital

Why GAO Did This Study

Hybrid capital instruments are securities that have characteristics of both equity and debt. The Federal Reserve allowed bank holding companies to include limited amounts of hybrid instruments known as trust preferred securities in the highest level of required capital (Tier 1), although other federal banking regulators never approved these or other hybrid instruments for this purpose. Responding to concerns that these instruments did not perform well during the 2007-2009 financial crisis, in 2010 the Dodd-Frank Wall Street Reform and Consumer Protection Act (Dodd-Frank Act) required regulators to establish rules that will exclude the instruments from Tier 1 capital and required GAO to study the possible effects of this provision. This report addresses (1) the use, benefits, and risks of hybrid instruments as Tier 1 capital; (2) the potential effects of the exclusion on banking institutions and the economy; and (3) options for smaller banking institutions to access regulatory capital. For this work, GAO analyzed data from financial regulatory filings and other sources, interviewed regulators and market participants, conducted economic analysis, and surveyed smaller banking institutions.

GAO makes no recommendations in this report. GAO provided a draft to the banking regulators for their review and comment. FDIC and the Federal Reserve provided technical comments that were incorporated, as appropriate.

View GAO-12-237. For more information, contact Thomas McCool at (202) 512-2642 or mccoolt@gao.gov.

What GAO Found

Tier 1 hybrid capital instruments, particularly trust preferred securities, have been heavily used by bank holding companies because of their financial advantages, but they are not as effective in absorbing losses as traditional forms of Tier 1 capital, such as common equity. As of December 31, 2010, almost two-thirds of all top-level bank holding companies that were subject to capital requirements included hybrid instruments in their Tier 1 capital, for a total value of $157 billion. Hybrid instruments such as trust preferred securities have offered institutions the benefit of lower-cost capital, largely because of their debt-related features— including tax-deductible dividends. These instruments also are accessible to a broader range of potential investors. However, trust preferred securities do not absorb losses like other Tier 1 instruments because of their obligation to repay principal and dividends. Trust preferred securities may provide limited financial flexibility in times of stress, but they may also hinder efforts to recapitalize troubled banking institutions.

Eliminating Tier 1 hybrid capital likely will have modest negative effects on the existing capital measures of individual banking institutions and lending and could improve institutions' financial stability. Few institutions will fall below minimum regulatory capital levels without Tier 1 hybrid instruments, and banking institutions' overall safety and soundness should improve with higher reliance on common equity. GAO's analysis of the relationship between bank regulatory capital and lending activity suggests that any negative effects on the cost and availability of credit should be small, but the exact impact is unknown. Market participants said that losing access to tax-advantaged Tier 1 instruments could place U.S. institutions at a competitive disadvantage, as some foreign banks may still have access to such instruments. The international competitive effects are unclear, however, given the scope of ongoing worldwide regulatory reforms.

Smaller banking institutions, which often had larger proportions of hybrid instruments as Tier 1 capital, have limited options for raising regulatory capital but indicated little unmet need for it. These smaller institutions now have access primarily to common equity raised from private sources. GAO's survey results showed that smaller institutions consider their financial condition and performance as the most important factor affecting their ability to raise capital. Market participants identified challenges that could impact smaller institutions' ability to raise capital, including limitations related to the size of capital raised, liquidity, and return potential for investors. However, GAO estimated that most smaller institutions (65 percent) had not raised regulatory capital since January 1, 2008, and of these, a large majority (88 percent) indicated that they had no need or interest in raising more. Further, most smaller institutions that had raised capital since 2008 were satisfied with the amount and terms involved. Only a small percentage of institutions (3 percent) that had attempted to raise capital since January 1, 2008, were unable to do so. Institutions with a stronger financial condition generally had a more favorable view of the capital raising environment.

Contents

Figures

Abbreviations

Basel Committee	Basel Committee on Banking Supervision
C&I	commercial and industrial loans
Dodd-Frank Act	Dodd-Frank Wall Street Reform and Consumer Protection Act
FDIC	Federal Deposit Insurance Corporation
Federal Reserve	Federal Reserve System
GDP	gross domestic product
IRS	Internal Revenue Service
OCC	Office of the Comptroller of the Currency
OLS	ordinary least squares
OTS	Office of Thrift Supervision
REIT	real estate investment trust
SEC	Securities and Exchange Commission
TARP	Troubled Asset Relief Program
VAR	vector autoregression

January 18, 2012

The Honorable Tim Johnson
Chairman
The Honorable Richard C. Shelby
Ranking Member
Committee on Banking, Housing,
    and Urban Affairs
United States Senate

The Honorable Spencer Bachus
Chairman
The Honorable Barney Frank
Ranking Member
Committee on Financial Services
House of Representatives

Capital is critical to banking institutions' ability to absorb unexpected losses and continue operating by making loans to businesses and consumers. Regulators require institutions to maintain certain levels of capital to promote stability across the banking industry and protect the nation's financial system. One type of capital is hybrid instruments, which have characteristics of both equity and debt. In 1996, the Board of Governors of the Federal Reserve System (Federal Reserve) began allowing bank holding companies to count a limited amount of certain hybrid instruments—known as trust preferred securities—as a portion of their Tier 1, or highest quality, capital.[1] Trust preferred securities offer tax advantages that make them cheaper than other forms of Tier 1 capital and as a result have been the most popular type of hybrid capital

---

[1]Tier 1 capital is considered the most stable and readily available capital that a banking institution can have to support its operations by absorbing unexpected financial losses. It consists of core capital elements, such as common stockholder's equity and noncumulative perpetual preferred stock. Other classes of capital include Tier 2, which consists of supplementary capital elements such as loan loss reserves, subordinated debt, and other instruments.

instrument.[2] At the end of 2009, their use was widespread, and bank holding companies held over $162 billion in hybrid instruments as part of required capital. In recent years, approximately two-thirds of bank holding companies and nearly all the largest bank holding companies have used hybrid instruments such as trust preferred securities to meet regulatory capital requirements. Smaller institutions have also relied on hybrid instruments issued jointly through pools to access needed capital.

However, regulators have not allowed depository institutions (banks and savings associations/thrifts) to use these types of hybrid instruments to meet Tier 1 capital requirements, including the Federal Reserve, the Federal Deposit Insurance Corporation (FDIC), the Office of the Comptroller of the Currency (OCC), and the Office of Thrift Supervision (OTS).[3] FDIC in particular has argued that trust preferred securities do not provide a degree of capital support consistent with Tier 1 capital status. Further, following the 2007-2009 financial crisis, some market participants and observers raised concerns that trust preferred securities and other hybrid instruments did not perform as well as other forms of capital in helping institutions withstand financial stress. In response, the Dodd-Frank Wall Street Reform and Consumer Protection Act (Dodd-Frank Act) of 2010 directed regulators to implement requirements that will effectively exclude most forms of hybrid instruments, including trust preferred securities, from Tier 1 capital for bank and thrift holding companies.[4] Specifically, Section 171 of the Dodd-Frank Act, also known as the Collins Amendment, requires banking regulators to establish rules that will subject certain bank holding companies to the same capital requirements that apply to insured depository institutions. The Dodd-Frank Act includes grandfathering and phase-in provisions for existing instruments, but because of the exclusions, trust preferred securities and other hybrid instruments issued on or after May 19, 2010, will no longer be a viable source of new Tier 1 capital for bank holding companies subject to Tier 1 capital requirements.

---

[2]Trust preferred securities are cumulative preferred stock instruments issued by a special-purpose entity (usually in the form of a trust) established by a bank holding company. The bank holding company issues subordinated debt to the special-purpose entity which uses the bank holding company's interest payments on the debt to make payments to the preferred stock investors.

[3]Section 313 of the Dodd-Frank Act abolished OTS, and section 312 distributed its regulatory functions among the Federal Reserve, FDIC, and OCC.

[4]Pub. L. No. 111-203, 124 Stat. 1376 (2010).

Some observers have had concerns about the potential impact that excluding hybrid instruments from Tier 1 capital may have on the cost and availability of credit and the international competitiveness of U.S. banking institutions. Additionally, concerns exist that the hybrid capital exclusion may limit access to regulatory capital for smaller institutions, many of which relied on pooled offerings of trust preferred securities as a unique form of access to public capital markets.[5] Section 174 of the Dodd-Frank Act required GAO to study banking institutions' use of hybrid capital instruments as a component of Tier 1 capital. In addition, Section 171 and Section 174 of the Dodd-Frank Act required us to study access to capital for smaller banking institutions. Accordingly, this report fulfills the two mandates by examining (1) the use of hybrid capital instruments as Tier 1 capital and the benefits and risks of including them in this category, (2) the potential effects on banking institutions and the economy of prohibiting the use of hybrid instruments to meet Tier 1 capital requirements, and (3) options that exist for smaller banking institutions to access regulatory capital.

To describe the regulatory use of Tier 1 hybrid capital instruments, we analyzed banking institutions' regulatory financial filings and reviewed the relevant federal banking regulations. To describe the benefits and risks of including hybrid instruments as Tier 1 capital, we reviewed studies from federal regulators, industry participants and observers, and academic sources. We conducted interviews with banking institutions, investment banks, credit rating agencies, law firms, industry associations, and each of the federal banking regulators. To evaluate the potential effects on banking institutions and the economy of prohibiting the use of hybrid instruments to meet Tier 1 capital requirements, we created a framework for our analysis that synthesized the findings and methodologies of existing studies on the economic and institutional effects of changes to bank capital requirements. We analyzed data on regulatory capital to determine the extent to which banking institutions may fall below minimum regulatory capital levels without Tier 1 hybrid instruments. We reviewed studies and compared U.S. regulatory policy with the international framework on hybrid capital proposed by the Basel

---

[5]The securities created from this pooling process, or securitization, were in the form of collateralized debt obligations (CDO), complex structured financial products involving a group of loans or debt securities that are pooled and used to issue securities in different tranches. These tranched CDO securities vary in risk and return depending on how the underlying cash flows produced by the pooled assets are allocated.

Committee on Banking Supervision. We also interviewed regulators, industry participants and observers, and European regulatory organizations to gather information on the possible effects of the hybrid capital exclusion on the international competitiveness of U.S. institutions. To examine the options that exist for smaller banking institutions to access capital, we conducted a nationally representative web-based survey of executives of banks, thrifts (savings associations), and bank and thrift holding companies with less than $10 billion in total assets. The survey identified their activities and experiences raising regulatory capital since January 1, 2008. The weighted response rate for this survey was 66 percent. All percentage estimates based on these survey results included in this report have a margin of error of plus or minus 7 percentage points or less. We also interviewed regulators and industry participants and observers regarding smaller institutions' options for and challenges associated with raising regulatory capital. To identify trends in the amount and types of regulatory capital raised since 2000, we analyzed Securities and Exchange Commission (SEC) data on public capital issuances. Appendixes I and II contain a more detailed discussion of our scope and methodology, and survey results can be found in appendix III.

For parts of our methodology that involved the analysis of computer-processed data, we assessed the reliability of these data and determined that they were sufficiently reliable for our purposes. Specifically, we accessed Federal Reserve regulatory capital data for holding companies and SEC capital issuance data through SNL Financial, a private data provider that collects information from a variety of sources and enters it into a proprietary database using standardized accounting templates. We conducted reliability assessments on the SNL Financial data and on thrift holding company data collected from OTS. To assess the reliability of these data, we reviewed factors such as the timeliness, accuracy, and completeness of data. We conducted electronic testing and manual review to identify missing and out-of-range data and other anomalies, and compared computer-generated data to source documents for a selected sample of companies.

We conducted this performance audit from December 2010 to January 2012 in accordance with generally accepted government auditing standards. Those standards require that we plan and perform the audit to obtain sufficient, appropriate evidence to provide a reasonable basis for our findings and conclusions based on our audit objectives. We believe that the evidence obtained provides a reasonable basis for our findings and conclusions based on our audit objectives.

Background

Capital reassures an institution's depositors, creditors, and counterparties that unanticipated losses or decreased earnings will not impair a financial institution's ability to repay its creditors or protect the savings of depositors. In general, capital represents the share of an institution's assets with no obligation for repayment, although this condition varies for less traditional forms of capital such as some hybrid instruments. Because capital generally does not have to be repaid, it can serve as a buffer against declines in asset values without subjecting an institution to default or insolvency. Capital typically is provided by a banking institution's owners or through earnings that are retained by the firm. When institutions experience financial losses, the value of the firm represented by the owner's stake (including retained earnings) is reduced first, thus protecting bank depositors and other creditors from loss.

Capital instruments vary in structure and their ability to absorb loss while preventing a banking institution from defaulting on its contractual repayment obligations. The strongest form of capital is common equity (or common stock), which carries no repayment obligation for principal or dividends, has the lowest payment priority in bankruptcy, and has no maturity date. Debt instruments are a weaker form of capital funding than common equity, as they require periodic interest payments and repayment of principal at maturity. Debt also has a higher claim than common equity in bankruptcy. Some debt instruments may qualify as capital if they contain certain equitylike characteristics such as a long maturity, subordination to other creditors, or ability to defer payments. Some hybrid instruments fall into this category, while others share more of the characteristics of common equity.

Three federal regulators oversee what we refer to as banking institutions in this report (that is, banks, savings associations (thrifts), and their holding companies). The Federal Reserve is the primary regulator for state-chartered member banks (i.e., state-chartered banks that are members of the Federal Reserve System) and bank and thrift holding companies. OCC is the primary regulator of federally chartered banks and thrifts, and FDIC is the primary regulator for state-chartered nonmember banks (i.e., state-chartered banks that are not members of the Federal Reserve System) and state-chartered thrifts. In addition, FDIC insures the deposits of all federally insured banks, generally up to $250,000 per depositor. Prior to July 21, 2011, OTS was the primary regulator of federally and state-chartered thrifts and thrift holding companies.

Because of capital's important role in absorbing losses, promoting confidence, and protecting depositors, federal banking law requires banking institutions to maintain adequate capital. Federal banking regulators set the minimum capital levels to ensure that the institutions they regulate maintain adequate capital. Federal law also authorizes banking regulators to take a variety of actions to ensure capital adequacy, including informal and formal enforcement actions. In implementing the statutory requirements, regulators generally expect institutions to hold capital at levels higher than regulatory minimums, with specific expectations based on institutions' risk profiles.

The United States, along with nearly all other major economies, agrees to comply with international capital standards set by the Basel Committee on Banking Supervision (the Basel Committee). The Basel Committee, which comprises representatives of central banks and banking regulators from 26 countries, issued its first set of international guidelines on bank capital (commonly known as "Basel I") in 1988. These guidelines included standards for the amount of capital banks should hold and the nature of the capital instruments that banks could count toward meeting these amounts. In 1998, the Basel Committee specified the characteristics of instruments that would either qualify as the highest quality (Tier 1) capital or would not meet this standard but could be eligible as lesser-quality (Tier 2) regulatory capital. For example, in order for instruments to be considered Tier 1 capital, the Basel Committee stated that instruments would need to meet certain criteria including deferability of dividends on a noncumulative basis, ability to absorb losses before the bank entered bankruptcy, permanence, and discretion over the amount and timing of distributions.[6] Common equity best meets all of the qualifications of Tier 1 capital and thus should comprise the predominant share of Tier 1 under Basel guidelines. The Basel Committee standards have been revised several times since 1988, including most recently with the Basel III reforms released in 2010.[7] Banking institutions subject to the Basel agreements are due to begin implementing some of the recently revised standards in 2013.

---

[6]Basel Committee on Banking Supervision press release, "Instruments eligible for inclusion in Tier 1 capital" (Oct. 27, 1998).

[7]For more information on prior revisions to Basel Committee capital standards, see GAO, *Risk-Based Capital: New Basel II Rules Reduced Certain Competitive Concerns, but Bank Regulators Should Address Remaining Uncertainties*, GAO-08-953 (Washington, D.C.: Sept. 12, 2008); and *Risk-Based Capital: Bank Regulators Need to Improve Transparency and Overcome Impediments to Finalizing the Proposed Basel II Framework*, GAO-07-253 (Washington, D.C.: Feb. 15, 2007).

GAO-12-237 Hybrid Capital Instruments

Regulatory Treatment of Hybrid Instruments

While definitions of hybrid capital vary, in this report we use "hybrid capital" and "hybrid instruments" to refer to those instruments that comprise what the Federal Reserve calls "restricted core capital elements": cumulative perpetual preferred stock, trust preferred securities, certain types of minority interest, and mandatory convertible trust preferred securities (see table 1).[8] These instruments include some but not all of the characteristics that the Basel Committee identified in 1998 as necessary for Tier 1 capital. Nonetheless, the Federal Reserve has allowed bank holding companies to include these instruments as Tier 1 capital.[9] Specifically, the Federal Reserve permits restricted core capital elements in Tier 1 capital in an amount of up to 25 percent of a bank holding company's total core capital elements after deducting goodwill.[10] Other than these hybrid instruments, the Federal Reserve subjects bank holding companies to capital requirements that are generally similar to those for depository institutions.[11] For example, in addition to common

---

[8]Restricted core capital also includes subordinated debt issued by bank holding companies electing to be taxed under Subchapter S of Chapter 1 of the Internal Revenue Code or bank holding companies organized in mutual form to the Department of the Treasury under the Troubled Asset Relief Program.

[9]The 1988 Basel I framework—which federal banking regulators adopted in 1989—introduced the Tier 1 capital category to internationally active banks. The Federal Reserve also voluntarily applied the standards to U.S. bank holding companies with the exception that holding companies could include the restricted core capital elements in Tier 1 capital on a limited basis. Although thrift holding companies also used hybrid capital instruments, OTS did not formally subject these institutions to uniform Tier 1 capital requirements but informally held them to similar standards as bank holding companies. For this purpose, OTS allowed thrift holding companies to include trust preferred securities in its proxy calculation of Tier 1 capital.

[10]The Federal Reserve defines core capital elements as common stockholders' equity, noncumulative perpetual preferred stock, a certain type of minority interest related to common or noncumulative perpetual preferred stock issued by a depository institution, and restricted core capital elements. Tier 1 capital includes the sum of core capital elements less intangible assets and other items. The Federal Reserve applied a 15 percent limit for large internationally active bank holding companies (generally those with greater than $250 billion in total assets), with an additional 10 percent allowed in the form of mandatory convertible trust preferred securities. Although the 15 percent restriction did not officially go into effect until 2011, agency officials said the Federal Reserve has informally requested that these large holding companies observe the limit since 1999.

[11]One type of restricted minority interest, known as Class C minority interest, relates to common equity and perpetual preferred shares issued by a nonbank consolidated subsidiary. Although the Federal Reserve considers this capital element as restricted core capital for bank holding companies, other bank regulators allow their supervised institutions to include this type of minority interest in Tier 1 if it relates to common equity and noncumulative perpetual preferred shares.

equity, all U.S. banking regulators recognize noncumulative perpetual preferred securities as a component of Tier 1 capital. Similarly, minority interests relating to common equity or noncumulative perpetual preferred securities are recognized as Tier 1 capital.

Table 1: Capital Instruments

Instrument	Definition
Common stock	Voting stock that represents ownership and does not have to be repaid. Dividend payments are not required unless declared and their amount is fully discretionary. Lowest priority in bankruptcy.
Noncumulative perpetual preferred stock	Nonvoting stock that represents ownership and does not have to be repaid. Entitles its holders to some preference or priority over the owners of common stock, usually regarding payment of dividends or asset distributions in a bankruptcy liquidation. Dividend payments are not required unless declared or made to holders of common stock. Dividend payment amounts are fixed but unpaid dividends do not accumulate. Lower bankruptcy priority than all capital instruments other than common stock.
Minority interest relating to common stock or noncumulative perpetual preferred stock issued by a consolidated subsidiary	Ownership by third-party investors of common or noncumulative perpetual preferred stock issued by a banking institution's subsidiary. The bank or bank holding company controls the subsidiary and consolidates the subsidiary on its balance sheet. The subsidiary may be a bank or nonbank entity.
Cumulative perpetual preferred stock	Nonvoting stock that represents ownership and does not have to be repaid. Entitles its holders to some preference or priority over the owners of common stock, usually regarding payment of dividends or asset distributions in a bankruptcy liquidation. Dividend payments are not required unless declared and payments are fixed. No common stock dividends can be paid until accumulated dividends are paid. Lower bankruptcy priority than all capital instruments other than common stock.
Minority interest relating to cumulative perpetual preferred stock issued by a consolidated subsidiary	Ownership by third-party investors of cumulative perpetual preferred stock issued by a banking institution's subsidiary. The bank or bank holding company controls the subsidiary and consolidates the subsidiary on its balance sheet. The subsidiary may be a bank or nonbank entity.
Trust preferred securities	Cumulative preferred stock issued by a special-purpose entity (usually in the form of a trust) established by a bank holding company. The bank holding company issues subordinated debt to the special-purpose entity, which uses the bank holding company's interest payments on the debt to make payments to the preferred stock investors. Dividends are required unless a negative declaration is made and unpaid dividends accrue.
Mandatory convertible trust preferred securities	A bank holding company jointly issues to investors trust preferred securities and a forward purchase contract that obligates the investors to purchase a fixed amount of the bank holding company's common stock, usually in 3 years. The investors place the trust preferred securities as collateral for the forward purchase contract. The common stock replaces the trust preferred securities as a component of the bank holding company's Tier 1 capital, and the trust preferred securities are excluded from its regulatory capital.

Source: GAO analysis of regulatory documents and other information.

As figure 1 illustrates, provisions in the Dodd-Frank Act require banking regulators to establish rules that will effectively subject bank and thrift holding companies to regulatory capital requirements that are at least as stringent as those applicable to insured depository institutions, thereby effectively eliminating hybrid capital instruments from Tier 1 capital. The restrictions will apply immediately to capital instruments issued on or after May 19, 2010. Only bank holding companies with less than $500 million in total assets are exempt from the Dodd-Frank Act hybrid capital exclusion.[12] Bank holding companies with between $500 million and $15 billion in total assets and thrift holding companies with less than $15 billion in total assets will be allowed to continue including hybrid instruments issued prior to May 19, 2010, in Tier 1 capital but may not use any hybrid instruments issued on or after that date. Bank and thrift holding companies with more than $15 billion in total assets will be required to phase out all of their Tier 1 hybrid capital issued prior to May 19, 2010, over a 3-year period from 2013 to 2016. The act subjects thrift holding companies to the same provisions as bank holding companies, except for thrift holding companies with less than $500 million in total assets. These institutions are treated the same as bank holding companies with between $500 million and $15 billion in total assets.

---

[12]For the purposes of this report, total assets refers to a holding company's total consolidated assets.

GAO-12-237 Hybrid Capital Instruments

Figure 1: Change in Tier 1 Eligibility of Capital Instruments Required by the Dodd-Frank Act

	Type of banking institution (regulator)			
	Bank holding companies[a]	Banks		
		Federally chartered banks and thrifts[b]	State-chartered banks that are not members of the Federal Reserve System and state-chartered thrifts[b]	State-chartered banks that are members of the Federal Reserve System
	(Federal Reserve)	(OCC)	(FDIC)	(Federal Reserve)
Common stock	✔	✔	✔	✔
Noncumulative perpetual preferred stock	✔	✔	✔	✔
Minority interest relating to common stock or noncumulative perpetual preferred stock issued by a consolidated subsidiary	✔[c]	✔	✔	✔
Cumulative perpetual preferred stock	✔[d]			
Trust preferred securities	✔[d]			
Minority interest relating to cumulative perpetual preferred stock issued by a consolidated subsidiary	✔[d]			
Mandatory convertible securities	✔[d]			

☐ Instrument not eligible for inclusion in Tier 1 capital pre- or post-Dodd Frank Act

✔ (outline) Instrument eligible for inclusion in Tier 1 capital pre-Dodd-Frank Act only

✔ (solid) Instrument eligible for inclusion in Tier 1 capital pre- and post-Dodd-Frank Act

Source: GAO

Notes: Does not include instruments issued pursuant to the Department of the Treasury's Troubled Asset Relief Program (TARP).

[a]Prior to July 21, 2011, the Office of Thrift Supervision (OTS) regulated thrift holding companies and did not formally subject these institutions to uniform capital requirements. However, OTS generally held thrift holding companies to similar standards as bank holding companies. On July 21, 2011, the Federal Reserve assumed regulatory responsibility for thrift holding companies.

[b]Prior to July 21, 2011, OTS was the primary regulator of federally and state-chartered thrifts.

[c]The amount eligible for Tier 1 capital is subject to limits if issued by a nondepository subsidiary.

[d]The amount eligible for Tier 1 capital is subject to limits.

Trust preferred securities have been the most common form of Tier 1 hybrid instrument among bank holding companies. The Internal Revenue Service (IRS) typically treats these securities as tax deductible, making them cheaper than other forms of Tier 1 capital. As figure 2 shows, the holding company establishes a special-purpose entity, usually in the form of a trust that holds all of the common equity. The trust issues undated cumulative preferred securities to outside investors and uses the proceeds to purchase a deeply subordinated unsecured note issued by the bank holding company.[13] Thus, the issuing trust serves as a conduit for exchanging funds between the bank holding company and the preferred equity investors. The subordinated note issued by the bank holding company is the trust's sole asset and is senior only to the bank holding company's common and preferred equity. The note has terms that generally replicate those of the trust preferred securities, except that the junior subordinated note has a fixed maturity of at least 30 years. Most trust agreements provide for the trust to terminate when the subordinated note matures. When the trust terminates, the trust preferred securities must be redeemed.

Figure 2: Framework of Trust Preferred Securities

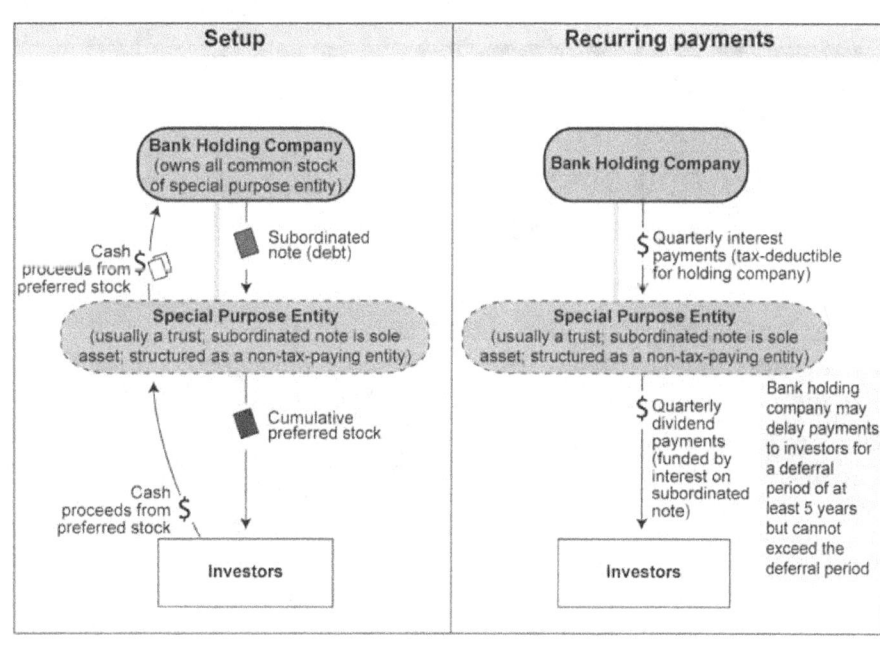

Source: GAO

---

[13]A subordinated note is a debt instrument that has a claim on assets junior to other debt and receives payment only after other debt with a more senior claim has been repaid.

The trust collects interest payments on the subordinated note from the bank holding company that it uses to pay dividends to holders of the trust preferred securities. The bank holding company can treat the interest payments on the subordinated note as a tax-deductible interest expense. The terms of the trust preferred securities allow dividends to be deferred for at least 5 years without creating an event of default or acceleration of the principal and accrued interest. After the 5-year dividend deferral period, if the trust fails to pay the cumulative dividend amount owed to investors, an event of default and acceleration occurs, giving investors the right to take the subordinated note issued by the bank holding company. At the same time, the bank holding company's obligation to pay principal and interest on the underlying junior subordinated note accelerates, and the note becomes immediately due and payable.

Hybrid Instruments, While Popular with Holding Companies, Do Not Absorb Losses Well

Bank Holding Companies Relied on Trust Preferred Securities for Tier 1 Hybrid Capital

Many bank holding companies have used hybrid instruments—predominantly trust preferred securities—to help meet Tier 1 capital requirements. In recent years, approximately two-thirds of all top-level bank holding companies that are subject to capital requirements (generally those with more than $500 million in total assets) have included hybrid instruments in their Tier 1 capital (see fig. 3).[14] For example, December 2010 data filed with the Federal Reserve showed that 85 percent of bank holding companies with more than $10 billion in total assets and 100 percent of bank holding companies with over $100

---

[14]For purposes of this report, top-level bank holding companies are defined as institutions that are not owned or controlled by other bank holding companies.

billion in total assets included hybrid instruments in their Tier 1 capital.[15] These hybrid instruments had a total value of $157 billion, representing 13 percent of all bank holding company Tier 1 capital. Of the total $157 billion in Tier 1 hybrid instruments, trust preferred securities accounted for $128 billion (82 percent).[16] Excluding the largest institutions with over $100 billion in total assets, trust preferred securities made up 97 percent of the total value of Tier 1 hybrid instruments.

---

[15]All top-level bank holding companies with total consolidated assets of $500 million or more and select bank holding companies with less than $500 million in total assets file annual financial statements with the Federal Reserve on form FR Y-9C, "Consolidated Financial Statements for Bank Holding Companies." Data from SNL Financial collected on July 11, 2011, showed that 973 top-level bank holding companies filed FR Y-9C regulatory capital data for 2010, of which 86 had less than $500 million in total assets. Additionally, the Federal Reserve has not required certain domestic subsidiaries of foreign banking institutions to meet capital requirements (for more on this policy, see GAO, *Bank Capital Requirements: Potential Effects of New Changes on Foreign Holding Companies and U.S. Banks Abroad,* GAO-12-160). These institutions, of which there were four by the end of 2010, are not included in our analyses. When discussing the use of hybrid capital instruments, we assume that institutions included the maximum amount of their reported elig ble hybrid instruments in Tier 1 up to the Federal Reserve's limit for their institution size.

[16]Mandatory convertible trust preferred securities, minority interest, and cumulative preferred securities accounted for the remaining 18 percent. See table 1 for descriptions of these instruments.

GAO-12-237 Hybrid Capital Instruments

Figure 3: Percentage of Top-Level Bank Holding Companies with Tier 1 Hybrid Instruments, 1997-2010

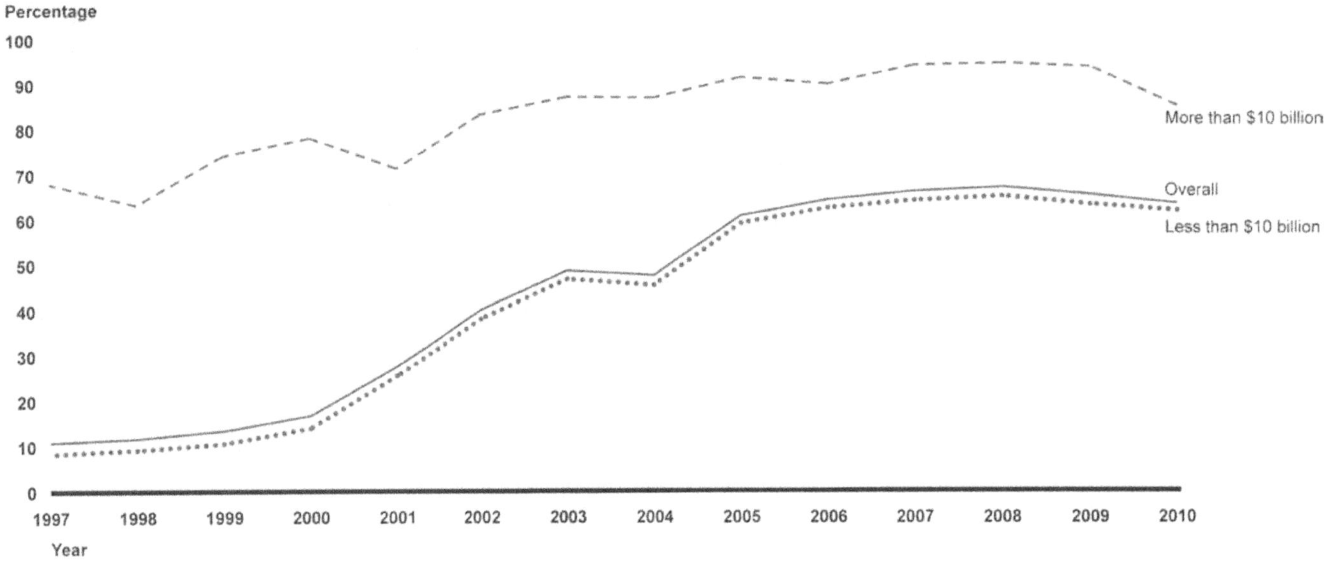

Percentage

Source: GAO analysis of Federal Reserve FR Y-9C data obtained from SNL Financial.

A few very large bank holding companies account for most of the value of all Tier 1 hybrid capital instruments. Specifically, the 20 largest bank holding companies with more than $100 billion in assets accounted for 85 percent of bank holding companies' Tier 1 hybrid capital as of December 2010 and the four largest companies accounted for over 50 percent. As figure 4 shows, the amount of hybrid instruments included in Tier 1 capital has grown significantly since 1997. Although the total amount grew as institutions' assets increased, the share of hybrid capital instruments in Tier 1 remained relatively consistent over time for the largest institutions. For example, in 1997, bank holding companies with more than $100 billion in total assets that included hybrid instruments in Tier 1 had a total of $6 billion of these instruments, or an average of 16 percent of the companies' total Tier 1 capital. By 2010, institutions of this size held $133 billion in hybrid instruments, but the average percentage of their total Tier 1 capital had fallen slightly to 14 percent.

Figure 4: Value of Hybrid Instruments in Bank Holding Company Tier 1 Capital, 1997-2010

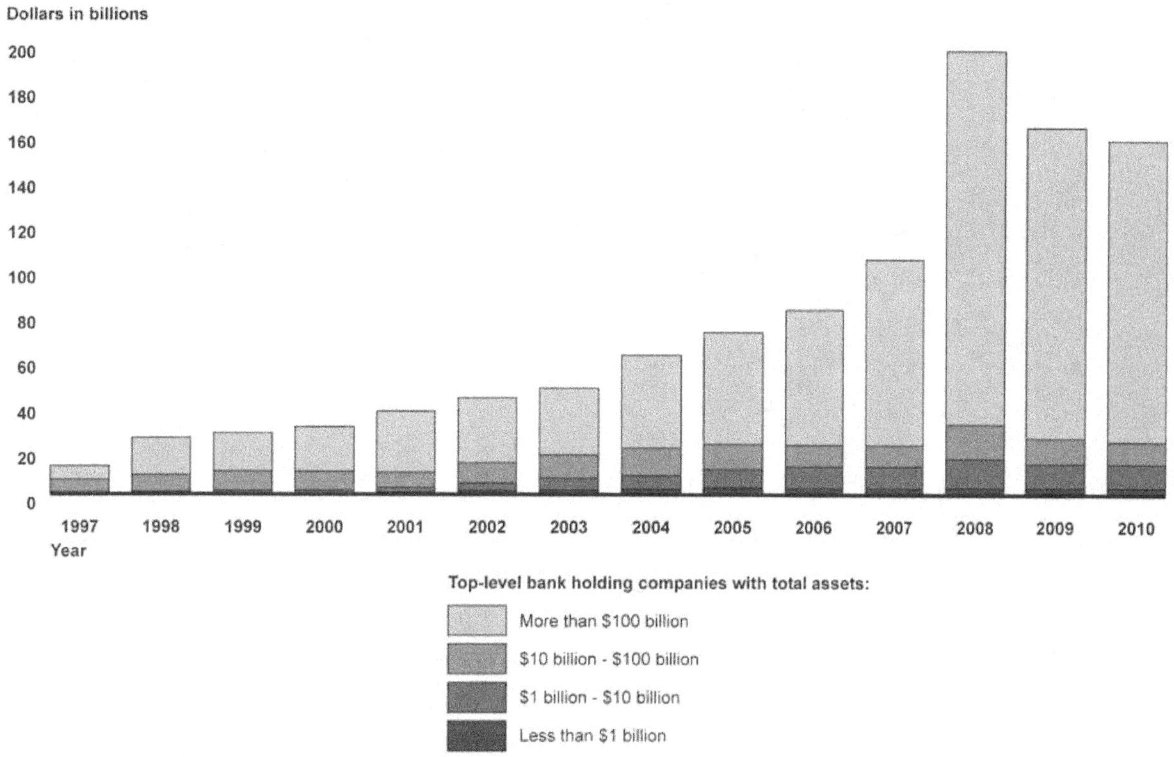

Dollars in billions

Top-level bank holding companies with total assets:

- More than $100 billion
- $10 billion - $100 billion
- $1 billion - $10 billion
- Less than $1 billion

Source: GAO analysis of Federal Reserve FR Y-9C data obtained from SNL Financial.

As figure 5 shows, among institutions that included hybrid instruments in their Tier 1 capital, institutions with less than $10 billion in assets have held, on average, a greater percentage of Tier 1 hybrid instruments than larger institutions—between 19 percent and 22 percent—in every year since 2000. By comparison, for larger bank holding companies, the percent of Tier 1 hybrid instruments averaged between 12 percent and 15 percent in all but 1 year over the same period.[17] One explanation for this difference may be that in 2005 the Federal Reserve had imposed a lower limit on the percentage of Tier 1 hybrid instruments that large,

---

[17]In 2008, hybrid instruments comprised an average of 20 percent of larger institutions' Tier 1 capital. This increase may be attributable to Troubled Asset Relief Program (TARP) investments in the largest banking institutions. Most of these investments in the largest institutions were made in the form of cumulative preferred securities.

internationally active institutions could hold than it imposed on smaller institutions.[18] Although this lower limit did not formally go into effect until March 2011, the Federal Reserve has informally requested that these institutions observe this limit since 1999, according to agency officials. As of December 2010, none of these institutions were using the maximum level of hybrid instruments allowed by the Federal Reserve for institutions of their size. By contrast, smaller institutions more frequently used the maximum amount of Tier 1 hybrid instruments allowed by the Federal Reserve. In 2010, 131 of the 558 smaller bank holding companies that included hybrid instruments in their Tier 1 capital included the maximum amount.

---

[18]Under a 2005 rule that came into effect in 2011, the Federal Reserve permitted large, internationally active institutions to include hybrid instruments in Tier 1 in the amount of up to 15 percent of total core capital elements after the deduction of goodwill. These institutions could also include up to an additional 10 percent in the form of mandatory convertible trust preferred securities. All other institutions were permitted to include hybrid instruments up to 25 percent of total core capital elements after the deduction of goodwill. Because under the prior rules the limits were calculated before the deduction of goodwill and because final Tier 1 capital generally includes additional deductions from total core capital elements for intangible assets and other items, some institutions included hybrid instruments at levels above 25 percent of Tier 1 capital.

GAO-12-237 Hybrid Capital Instruments

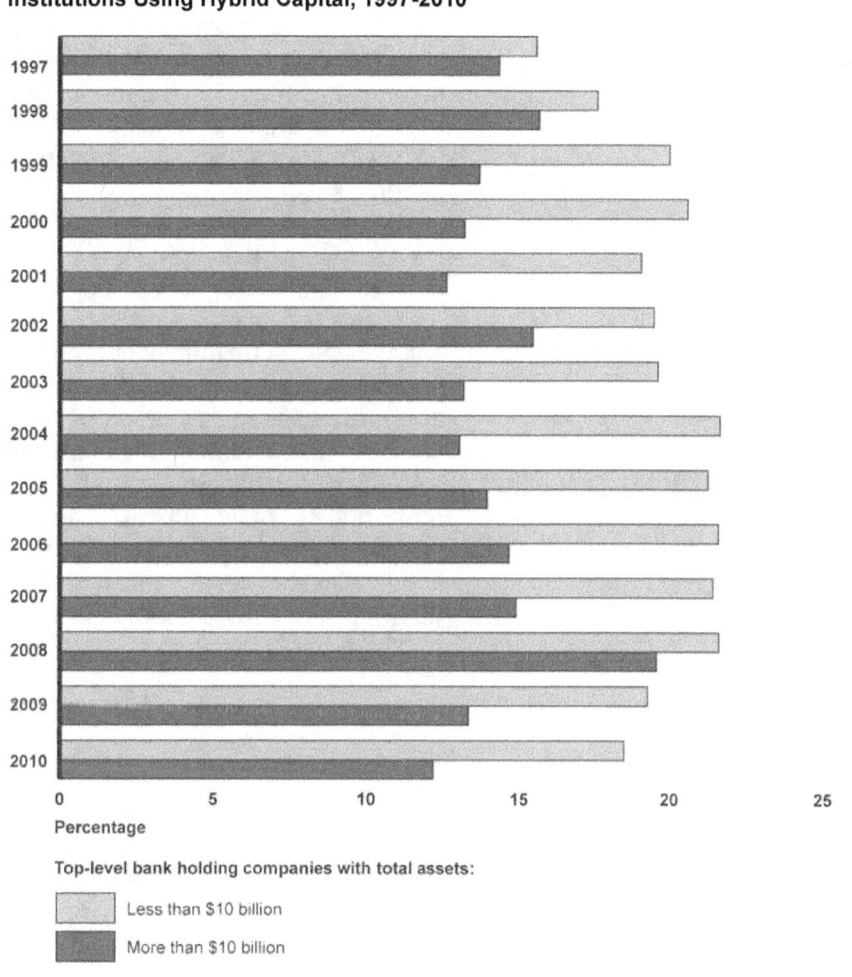

Figure 5: Average Percentage of Tier 1 Capital Held in Hybrid Instruments by Institutions Using Hybrid Capital, 1997-2010

Top-level bank holding companies with total assets:

☐ Less than $10 billion

■ More than $10 billion

Source: GAO analysis of Federal Reserve FR Y-9C data obtained from SNL Financial.

Fewer Thrift Holding Companies Have Used Trust Preferred Securities

Compared to bank holding companies, fewer thrift holding companies have used trust preferred securities. Prior to the transfer of supervisory authority under the Dodd-Frank Act, thrift holding companies were supervised by OTS and were not subject to a uniform Tier 1 capital requirement. However, OTS examiners did consider use of trust preferred securities when monitoring thrift holding companies' capital adequacy. For example, examiners used a proxy calculation that included trust preferred securities to approximate a Tier 1 capital measure and, consistent with Federal Reserve rules, generally recognized only a portion of these securities as the highest-quality capital.[19] The number of thrift holding companies using trust preferred securities peaked in 2006 at 132 of 473, or 28 percent of all thrift holding companies.[20] By comparison, in the same year, 64 percent of bank holding companies included trust preferred securities in their Tier 1 capital. As of December 31, 2010, only 95 of 434 thrift holding companies (22 percent) used trust preferred securities.

Unlike bank holding companies, whose use of trust preferred securities has remained relatively consistent since 2008, the amount of trust preferred securities that thrift holding companies have used has declined substantially in recent years (see fig. 6). Specifically, thrift holding companies' use of trust preferred securities peaked at $21 billion in 2007 but had declined to $3 billion by the end of 2010. In part, this decline came about because many of the largest users of trust preferred securities had failed or reorganized. As with bank holding companies, a small number of institutions accounted for a large share of the total amount of trust preferred securities held by thrift holding companies, with just five institutions accounting for more than 70 percent in 2007. By 2010, all of these companies were no longer thrift holding companies due to failure or reorganization.

---

[19]We are considering only thrift holding companies' use of trust preferred securities rather than hybrid instruments more generally. The Thrift Financial Report schedule for holding companies did not include a separate line item for cumulative preferred instruments prior to 2009. OTS did include minority interest in its proxy Tier 1 capital calculation, but OTS data do not distinguish between minority interest that would have been restricted by the Federal Reserve for bank holding companies and minority interest that would have been unrestricted and still included as Tier 1 capital under the Dodd-Frank Act.

[20]We consider thrift holding companies to have used trust preferred securities in a given year if the companies reported them on their Thrift Financial Report holding company schedule for that year. Amounts of trust preferred securities listed for thrift holding companies include only the amount that would be eligible for Tier 1 capital treatment under the Federal Reserve's rules for bank holding companies.

GAO-12-237 Hybrid Capital Instruments

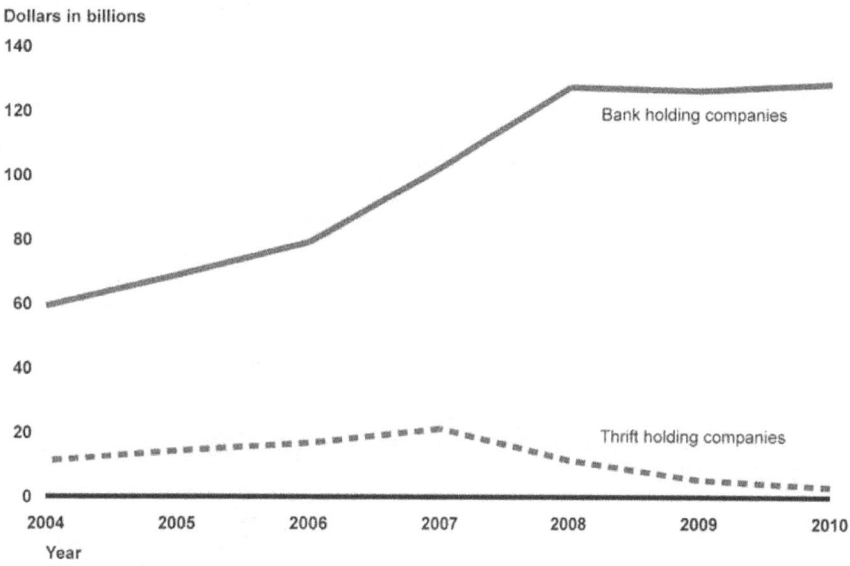

Figure 6: Amount of Trust Preferred Securities Eligible for Tier 1 Capital Treatment under the Federal Reserve's Rules for Bank Holding Companies, 1997-2010

Source: GAO analysis of Thrift Financial Report data obtained from OTS and Federal Reserve FR Y-9C data obtained from SNL Financial.

Note: Data on thrift holding company use of trust preferred securities is not available prior to 2004, when OTS added the field for trust preferred securities in its Thrift Financial Report.

Hybrid Instruments Offer Financial Advantages but Are a Weaker Form of Tier 1 Capital

Hybrid capital instruments have provided financial advantages to the banking institutions that have used them but are a lower-quality form of Tier 1 capital than other financial instruments. Trust preferred securities, the predominant form of Tier 1 hybrid capital, offered institutions a low-cost form of capital primarily because of their debtlike features, including tax-deductible payments. Unlike dividends on traditional preferred and common stock, dividends on trust preferred securities are treated as tax deductible because the bank holding company makes interest payments on the subordinated note held by the trust. Deducting dividend or interest payments for tax purposes can lower an institution's overall capital cost and increase after-tax earnings (see fig. 7). In addition, trust preferred securities generally offered a cheaper source of Tier 1 capital than common or noncumulative preferred equity because of other debtlike features, including an effective maturity date, cumulative dividend payments, and a superior repayment claim in case of bankruptcy or liquidation.

Figure 7: Illustrative Cost-Benefit Example of Trust Preferred Securities

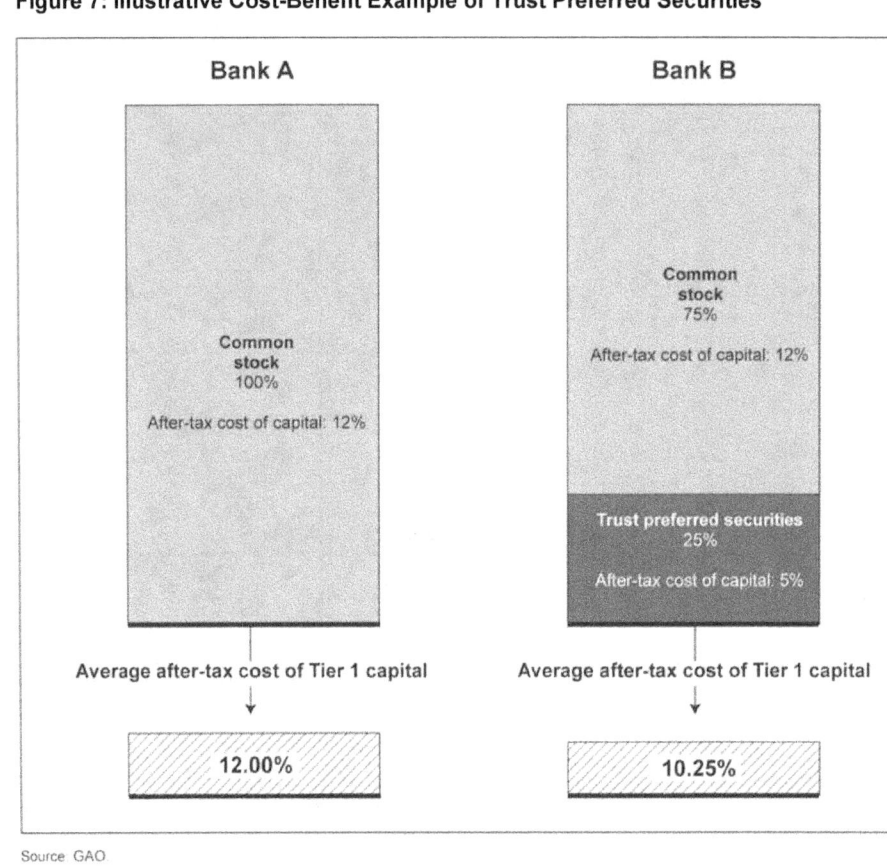

Source: GAO

Note: The cost of capital figures for common stock and trust preferred securities are hypothetical assumptions and are not based on observed prices. Cost of capital refers to the amount an institution must pay the owners of capital for its use, including the costs of interest payments on debt and dividends generated for shareholders.

Banking institutions also have used trust preferred securities to increase financial returns to existing shareholders. For example, because trust preferred securities are not equity of the banking institution and do not dilute the ownership stakes of existing common shareholders, bank holding companies have leveraged these instruments by using them as a capital source to fund lending and other activity. As a result, the holding companies could increase returns on common equity and earnings per common share—two important measures for investors. These effects are similar to those that can be achieved with debt financing or by issuing preferred stock. However, because payments on trust preferred securities are tax deductible, they are a more efficient means for achieving these effects. Also, trust preferred securities' debtlike features have allowed institutions to raise capital from a larger group of potential investors that faced restrictions on investments in other Tier 1 capital instruments. For example, market participants said that trust preferred securities offered banking institutions access to investors in fixed-income assets that make up a larger market than equity investors. Finally, according to one market participant, trust preferred securities were attractive to investors who did not want to face bank holding company restrictions by exceeding ownership limits, because they did not include the ownership rights of directly issued equity instruments such as common and preferred stock.

However, trust preferred securities lack many characteristics of higher-quality capital, such as common equity. Common equity is the highest-quality capital instrument for absorbing losses and maintaining the ongoing financial viability of banking institutions. Market participants and bank regulators generally recognize common equity as the strongest form of capital, and regulators require banking institutions to have most of their Tier 1 capital as common equity. In the stressed market conditions of the recent financial crisis, market participants focused on common equity when assessing the strength of banking institutions. Several characteristics make common equity such an effective capital instrument for absorbing unexpected financial losses that could otherwise threaten the ongoing viability of a banking institution. These include an unrestricted ability to absorb losses while the institution continues to operate as a going concern, full discretion over payments to holders, and permanence. Other Tier 1 instruments share these attributes to a varying extent. For example, noncumulative preferred shares eligible for Tier 1 status have a perpetual maturity and no obligation to make dividend payments. However, these instruments are more limited in their ability to absorb losses as they may do so only after losses reduce the sum of common stock and surplus and retained earnings below zero.

In contrast, trust preferred securities do not contain features that allow them to absorb financial losses outside of bankruptcy. Issuers of the instruments have a contractual obligation to repay the full principal amount and all dividends, and failure to repay at the maturity of the note may result in default. Market participants said that some large institutions had been able to absorb financial losses by exchanging existing securities, but at a discount, and not as a feature of the instruments.[21] However, the instruments do not contain any contractual rights to such transactions, and any discount depends on a voluntary renegotiation of the security in light of an institution's financial distress, as investors cannot be forced to exchange them. As a result, credit rating agencies identify some exchanges as distressed, which they consider to be a default event that could threaten a banking institution's viability. According to one market participant, exchanges were an option for only relatively strong troubled banks because investors received common equity and would agree to convert only if they were reasonably confident that the banking institution would survive.

Trust preferred securities also do not allow for complete discretion over dividend or principal payments, although they may provide some limited financial flexibility in times of stress. Institutions' ability to defer dividend payments for up to 5 years may help institutions withstand financial stress by preserving cash for other purposes.[22] However, institutions face limits on the benefits they receive from dividend deferrals. For example, missed dividend payments accumulate and the issuer has a contractual obligation to pay the missed amounts in full by the end of the deferral period or be subject to default. Thus, dividend deferrals cannot increase an institution's earnings or the amount of its equity capital but instead offer only temporary flexibility in the use of its cash funds. This flexibility is limited by the relatively small size of dividend payments, which constitute only a small share of an instrument's principal value, so that realizing significant benefits from deferring dividend payments is difficult.

Troubled institutions are often reluctant to defer dividend payments.[23] Market participants and some regulators we interviewed identified the

---

[21]If an investor exchanges existing trust preferred securities for a discounted amount of another capital instrument, such as common equity, issued by the same institution or sells the trust preferred securities back to the institution for less than the investor paid for them, the transaction increases the institution's capital by extinguishing a liability.

[22]For inclusion in Tier 1 capital, the Federal Reserve has required trust preferred securities to allow for the deferral of dividend payments for up to a minimum of 20 consecutive quarters without an event of default. Although the dividend deferral period could be longer, 5 years was the typical time frame included in the securities' contracts.

[23]Banking regulators also can force institutions to defer dividends on trust preferred securities if they believe it is necessary to help preserve the institution's safety and soundness.

GAO-12-237 Hybrid Capital Instruments

negative consequences for institutions that defer dividends on their trust preferred securities. Investors' expectations about receiving dividends can place pressure on institutions to keep paying. An institution's decision to defer dividends on trust preferred securities, as with common stock and other instruments, can send additional negative signals to investors and other market participants about its financial strength. To the extent that investors view deferral as a sign of financial weakness, deferring dividends can limit an institution's ability to raise capital and increase the cost of any subsequent capital-raising efforts. According to market participants, some banking institutions that could have benefited from deferring payments during the financial crisis did not do so because of such concerns. Market participants also said that larger, publicly traded institutions have been more reluctant to defer dividends than smaller institutions. One reason for their reluctance is that these institutions may decide that the consequences of deferral for their common stock prices would be too detrimental. Larger institutions also tend to rely more heavily on access to capital markets as a source of funding and can be more reluctant than smaller institutions to jeopardize their access to these markets in the future. According to Federal Reserve officials, these consequences are secondary to the consequences of an institution eliminating common stock dividends, a step an institution must take before it can defer dividends on perpetual preferred stock or trust preferred securities and one that has significant market implications for the institution.

Few institutions that have deferred dividend payments have recovered and paid the accumulated amount of the deferrals. Some market participants said that the length of the dividend deferral period is long enough for an institution to either recover or fail by the time all accrued payments become due. Available data on the outcome of deferring dividends on trust preferred securities indicate that most banking institutions have not recovered but remain in deferral or have defaulted. According to a leading credit rating agency, of the 605 banking institutions in pooled trust preferred securities that have deferred dividends since January 1, 2007, some 62 percent are still deferring, 29 percent have defaulted, and 7 percent had repaid all missed dividends as of September

30, 2011.[24] Another leading credit rating agency found a similar trend.[25] However, limited historical data exist on such deferrals, because most institutions issued the securities after 2000, and banking institutions operated in a favorable economic environment until the 2007-2009 financial crisis.

Trust preferred securities also differ from stronger Tier 1 capital instruments because they are not a permanently available capital source. A perpetual maturity is a strong feature because it helps ensure that capital will be available to absorb losses when needed and that the institution will not have to repay or replace funds used as capital. Unlike common equity and other Tier 1 instruments, trust preferred securities have an effective maturity date when the principal amount must be repaid. In the typical trust preferred security structure, the subordinated note issued by the bank holding company has a maturity of at least 30 years, and maturity cannot be perpetual in order to qualify for tax deductibility. In most cases, the trust terminates at the maturity of the subordinated note, and the trust preferred securities must be redeemed.

Finally, trust preferred securities can hinder the recapitalization of troubled banking institutions. Some market participants and regulators said that the existence of trust preferred securities can act as an impediment to improving an institution's capital structure—or recapitalization. An institution that is deferring dividends on trust preferred securities cannot pay dividends to common or preferred stockholders until all accumulated dividends have been paid. As a result, investors may require an exchange of trust preferred securities for equity or a reduction in their principal amount before investing new equity, and reaching agreement on such an exchange or reduction can be difficult. Any funds

---

[24]Seven of the institutions (about 1 percent) had their deferring securities sold or otherwise disposed of by the pooled entity. Data are from Fitch Ratings' *Bank Default and Deferral Index,* which tracks defaults and deferrals by banking institutions whose securities make up the 85 pooled trust preferred securities rated by Fitch (originated value of $37.7 billion for around 1,800 institutions). The *Bank Default and Deferral Index* data also include a very small amount of senior and subordinated debt, but Fitch officials said that essentially all of the deferral data was for trust preferred securities. Fitch typically characterizes a deferral as a banking institution that has elected to defer payments on its trust preferred securities or similar debt instrument and considers defaulted institutions those that have been closed by bank regulators or that have filed for bankruptcy.

[25]Moody's Investors Service, *TRUP CDOs: 2011 Outlook and 2010 Year in Review* (New York, NY: Jan. 13, 2011).

from new equity investments would first be used to pay the accumulated dividends before paying dividends on common stock or other equity. Holders of trust preferred securities have reduced incentives to subordinate their position in a recapitalization because they have legal rights to cumulative dividends and the repayment of principal. Also, the structure of pooled trust preferred securities—typically a collateralized debt obligation (CDO)—can impede the approval of transactions to exchange the securities for equity or repurchase them at a discounted price. For example, market participants said it can be difficult to identify and gain approval for recapitalization transactions from the ultimate CDO investors. If a trustee represents the CDO investors, the trustee often will not agree to a proposed transaction or will require a very high percentage of the investors to agree because of concerns about potential legal liability.

Excluding Tier 1 Hybrid Capital Likely Will Have Limited Negative Effects

With the exclusion of hybrid instruments from Tier 1, few banking institutions will fall below minimum amounts of regulatory capital, and greater reliance on common equity should improve the overall safety and soundness of banking institutions. To identify and resolve problems at banks and thrifts, the prompt corrective action provisions require depository institution regulators to classify insured depository institutions into one of five capital categories—well capitalized, adequately capitalized, undercapitalized, significantly undercapitalized, and critically undercapitalized—using different capital measures. Among these are the Tier 1 risk-based capital ratio (Tier 1 ratio), which measures Tier 1 capital as a share of risk-weighted assets and the Tier 1 leverage ratio (leverage ratio), which measures Tier 1 capital as a share of average total consolidated assets.[26] Well-capitalized banks have a Tier 1 ratio of 6 percent or more, adequately capitalized banks a ratio of 4 percent or more, and undercapitalized banks a ratio of less than 4 percent.[27] The minimum leverage ratio is 4 percent for most banks, and well-capitalized

---

[26]Risk-weighted assets are on- and off-balance sheet assets adjusted for their risk characteristics. The other measures are the total risk-based capital ratio and a fourth measure that regulators use to identify critically undercapitalized institutions. We use the Tier 1 risk-based and leverage ratios to measure institutions' capital adequacy, as these ratios would be most directly affected by the Tier 1 hybrid capital restrictions.

[27]To be well capitalized, a bank must meet the criteria for all three capital measures, and banks may be considered undercapitalized if they fail to meet adequately capitalized criteria for any of the measures.

banks have a leverage ratio of 5 percent or more. The Federal Reserve applies similar minimum levels when assessing the capital adequacy of bank holding companies but generally does not identify specific criteria for adequately or well-capitalized institutions or use the term undercapitalized (see table 2).[28]

Table 2: Banking Institution Capital Requirements

	Tier 1 risk-based capital ratio	Tier 1 leverage ratio
Banks and thrifts		
Well capitalized	6% or more	5% or more
Adequately capitalized	4% or more	4% or more[a]
Undercapitalized	Less than 4%	Less than 4%[a]
Bank holding companies		
Above minimum capital	4% or more	4% or more[b]
Below minimum capital	Less than 4%	Less than 4%

Sources: FDIC—12 C.F.R. § 325.103 and § 390.453; Federal Reserve—12 C F R. § 208.43 and 12 C.F.R. Part 225, appendixes A and D; and OCC—12 C F R. § 6.4 and § 165.4.

Notes: As noted, the Dodd-Frank Act transfers to OCC the functions of OTS relating to federal savings associations and transfers to FDIC the functions of OTS relating to state savings associations. Section 316 of the Dodd-Frank Act requires that OCC and the FDIC identify those regulations of the OTS that are continued and that they will enforce. Both OCC and OTS listed OTS's prompt corrective action regulations, 12 C.F.R. Part 565, as among the regulations that they will enforce. *See* 75 Fed. Reg. 39246, 39247-39248.

[a]The minimum leverage ratio is 3 percent for banks or thrifts that have the strongest supervisory examination ratings and that generally are not experiencing or anticipating significant growth.

[b]The minimum leverage ratio is 3 percent for bank holding companies with the strongest supervisory examination ratings and those that are subject to a risk-based capital measure for market risk.

We evaluated the impact of the Tier 1 hybrid capital exclusion on bank holding companies' capital levels using the explicit criteria for well capitalized that apply to banks and thrifts and found that most bank holding companies would experience a reduction in Tier 1 capital but maintain well-capitalized status without Tier 1 hybrids. Of the 969 top-level bank holding companies filing consolidated regulatory financial

---

[28]The minimum leverage ratio is 3 percent for bank holding companies with the strongest examination ratings and those that have implemented a risk-based capital measure for market risk. For all other bank holding companies, the minimum leverage ratio is 4 percent. We evaluated all bank holding companies using the higher minimum requirement. The Federal Reserve defines well capitalized for certain bank holding companies, including those under $500 million in total assets that are subject to its Small Bank Holding Company Policy Statement.

GAO-12-237 Hybrid Capital Instruments

reports for 2010, 615 had hybrid instruments that the Dodd-Frank Act would exclude from Tier 1 capital.[29] However, the amount of other Tier 1 capital instruments was large enough that 587 (95 percent) of these institutions would see no change in the capital adequacy category of their Tier 1 ratio without those instruments. As table 3 shows, 554 (90 percent) would maintain a Tier 1 ratio of well capitalized.[30] The average Tier 1 ratio of all top-level bank holding companies would fall from 13.5 percent to 12.2 percent after excluding Tier 1 hybrid instruments, and the average ratio of institutions with Tier 1 hybrids would decrease by around 2 percentage points but remain considerably higher than the minimum level for the well-capitalized category.

Table 3: Tier 1 Ratio Capital Categories of Top-Level Bank Holding Companies with Tier 1 Hybrids, as of December 31, 2010

Total asset size	Number of institutions	Tier 1 hybrid instruments	Average Tier 1 ratio	Well capitalized	Above minimum[a]	Below minimum
More than $15 billion	44	Included	13.1%	44	0	0
		Excluded	11.6%	44	0	0
Between $500 million and $15 billion[b]	526	Included	12.7%	500	11	15
		Excluded	10.6%	485	20	21
Less than $500 million[c]	45	Included	9.0%	30	6	9
		Excluded	7.1%	25	9	11
Total	**615**	**Included**	**12.5%**	**574**	**1/**	**24**
		Excluded	**10.4%**	**554**	**29**	**32**

Source: GAO analysis of Federal Reserve data obtained from SNL Financial.

[a]The above minimum category does not include institutions in the category we refer to as well capitalized.

[b]Tier 1 hybrid instruments excluded for illustrative purposes. Institutions with less than $15 billion of total assets can continue including hybrid instruments issued prior to May 19, 2010, in Tier 1 capital.

[c]Tier 1 hybrid instruments excluded for illustrative purposes. Institutions with less than $500 million of total assets are largely exempt from the Dodd-Frank Act exclusion of Tier 1 hybrid capital.

While the Dodd-Frank Act includes exemptions from the Tier 1 hybrid capital exclusion for the two categories of smaller institutions, our analysis

---

[29]Our analyses do not include four top-level holding companies that are subsidiaries of foreign banking institutions and were exempt from Tier 1 regulatory capital requirements in 2010.

[30]Of the 941 that would have no change in their capital adequacy category, 587 had Tier 1 hybrid instruments as of December 31, 2010.

revealed that some smaller institutions with Tier 1 hybrid instruments would not fare as well as larger institutions if they had to exclude hybrid instruments from Tier 1 capital. Specifically, 20 institutions would see the capital category of their Tier 1 ratio fall below the well-capitalized criteria but remain above the minimum level, and an additional 8 would fall to below the minimum level. All of these institutions had less than $2.5 billion in total assets and 7 had less than $500 million as of December 31, 2010. The average Tier 1 ratio of these 28 institutions, including Tier 1 hybrid instruments, was well below the overall average at 6.3 percent and would fall to 4.7 percent without Tier 1 hybrid instruments.

Our analysis also found that more institutions would not meet the higher minimum Tier 1 ratio under Basel III, particularly smaller firms. However, how U.S. regulators will implement Basel III is unclear, including how they will determine which institutions will have to meet the higher standards or set the time frames for implementation. The Basel III capital framework—which all member countries, including the United States, have approved—increases the Tier 1 capital ratio and excludes the same hybrid instruments from Tier 1 as the Dodd-Frank Act.

Effects of the hybrid capital exclusion on institutions' leverage ratio capital categories would also be modest, although more institutions would fall below minimum levels. Almost all of the 615 institutions with Tier 1 hybrid capital would be in the same category of leverage ratio capital without those instruments. For example, about the same number of institutions would maintain Tier 1 and leverage ratios of well capitalized (see table 4). However, leverage ratios for 20 institutions would fall below the minimum level.[31] All of the institutions that would see their leverage ratio capital categories fall had less than $4 billion in total assets and 9 had less than $500 million as of December 31, 2010. After excluding Tier 1 hybrid instruments, the average leverage ratio for all top-level bank holding companies would fall from 9.2 percent to 8.2 percent. The average ratio of institutions with Tier 1 hybrids would decrease from 8.9 percent to 7.3 percent, also considerably higher than the minimum level for the well-capitalized category.

---

[31]We used a leverage ratio requirement of 4 percent for all institutions. However, the Federal Reserve allows some bank holding companies to meet the leverage ratio requirement with a ratio of 3 percent based on their examination ratings and other factors.

Table 4: Leverage Ratio Capital Categories of Top-Level Bank Holding Companies with Tier 1 Hybrid Instruments, as of December 31, 2010

Total asset size	Number of institutions	Tier 1 hybrid instruments	Average leverage ratio	Well capitalized	Above minimum[a]	Below minimum
More than $15 billion	44	Included	9.0%	44	0	0
		Excluded	8.0%	44	0	0
Between $500 million and $15 billion[b]	526	Included	9.0%	493	11	22
		Excluded	7.5%	472	19	35
Less than $500 million[c]	45	Included	6.6%	26	6	13
		Excluded	5.2%	23	2	20
Total	**615**	**Included**	**8.9%**	**563**	**17**	**35**
		Excluded	**7.3%**	**539**	**21**	**55**

Source: GAO analysis of Federal Reserve data obtained from SNL Financial.

[a]The above minimum category does not include institutions in the category we refer to as well capitalized.

[b]Tier 1 hybrid instruments excluded for illustrative purposes. Bank holding companies with less than $15 billion of total assets can continue including hybrid instruments issued prior to May 19, 2010, in Tier 1 capital.

[c]Tier 1 hybrid instruments excluded for illustrative purposes. Bank holding companies with less than $500 million of total assets are largely exempt from the Dodd-Frank Act exclusion of Tier 1 hybrid capital.

Exceptions to the hybrid exclusion will help limit potential negative effects on institutions' capital levels. For example, as discussed earlier, the Dodd-Frank Act includes grandfathering provisions for bank holding companies with less than $15 billion in total assets that will allow these institutions to continue including hybrid instruments issued before May 19, 2010, in Tier 1 capital. Thus, all of these institutions that would have had their capital adequacy categories reduced based on their year-end 2010 Tier 1 or leverage ratios will not experience a reduction in Tier 1 levels as a result of the hybrid capital exclusion.[32] Furthermore, as discussed earlier, the Dodd-Frank Act largely exempts institutions with less than

---

[32]This finding assumes that institutions had not issued Tier 1 hybrid capital between May 19, 2010, and December 31, 2010. The Senate adopted the Collins Amendment in May 2010, and it became law when the Dodd-Frank Act was passed in July 2010.

$500 million in total assets from the exclusion of Tier 1 hybrid capital.[33] In addition, although none of the larger bank holding companies not subject to the grandfathering provisions would fall below minimum capital levels or experience a reduction in capital categories based on the Tier 1 ratio or leverage ratio, a phase-in period will help limit the immediate effects of the hybrid capital exclusion. For institutions with $15 billion or more in total assets, hybrid capital deductions from Tier 1 must be phased in over 3 years beginning on January 1, 2013, almost 2-1/2 years after passage of the Dodd-Frank Act.

Further, increased reliance on stronger forms of capital should increase institutions' financial stability. Some institutions may have difficulty replacing hybrid instruments or choose not to replace them with other forms of Tier 1 capital. But to the extent that banking institutions replace hybrid capital instruments with capital that has a higher capacity to absorb unexpected losses—such as common equity—institutions' financial resiliency should improve. Some market participants identified likely safety and soundness benefits for banking institutions that increase their share of common equity or other stronger capital sources. A few market participants noted that some institutions may respond to increased capital costs by increasing lending and investment risks, including activities for which increased risk may not require additional capital under existing risk-based capital requirements, to generate higher returns. However, bank regulators have the discretion to require higher levels of capital for institutions with heightened risk profiles, and recent Basel Committee reforms include enhancing the risk coverage of the capital framework by strengthening capital requirements for trading activities, complex securitization exposures, and counterparty credit exposures.

One market participant argued that the safety and soundness effects could be negative if institutions decided to hold less capital overall rather than increasing the share of common equity. Another market participant noted that the hybrid capital exclusion limits institutions' options for raising

---

[33]The Collins Amendment provisions in the Dodd-Frank Act do not apply to any institutions subject to the Federal Reserve's Small Bank Holding Company Policy Statement that was in effect on May 19, 2010. This statement generally applies to all bank holding companies with less than $500 million in total assets that (1) are not engaged in significant nonbanking activities, (2) do not conduct significant off-balance sheet activities, and (3) do not have a material amount of debt or equity securities outstanding (other than trust preferred securities) that are registered with the Securities and Exchange Commission. The Dodd-Frank Act did not similarly exempt small thrift holding companies.

capital in times of financial distress. However, institutions that decide not to replace Tier 1 hybrid capital could retain the instruments in their capital structure, and the hybrid capital may qualify as Tier 2 capital. Furthermore, institutions will still be required to have capital levels sufficient to support safety and soundness, and this capital will be higher quality that will better absorb unexpected losses and improve institutions' ability to withstand periods of financial distress.

Effects on the Cost and Availability of Credit Likely Will Be Small

The exclusion of hybrid instruments from Tier 1 capital likely will have modest immediate and long-term effects on the cost and availability of credit. In general, the hybrid capital exclusion could negatively affect the cost and availability of credit in two ways. First, if institutions view their Tier 1 capital positions as insufficient without existing hybrid instruments, they may take actions to maintain consistent regulatory capital levels, creating a negative capital shock that empirical studies suggest could have an impact on lending activity. For example, institutions could choose to replace excluded hybrid capital with other Tier 1 instruments such as common equity, increase capital through retained earnings, or reduce risk-weighted assets. Second, regardless of whether institutions take such actions, those that had previously relied on Tier 1 hybrid instruments as a cheaper form of capital could experience higher overall capital costs when raising Tier 1 capital in the future. Loan rates could increase if institutions choose to and are able to pass on any increased capital costs to borrowers.

Short-Term Effects of Maintaining Tier 1 Capital Positions without Hybrid Instruments

The terms of the hybrid capital exclusion and the relationship between lending activity and changes to capital levels will limit the exclusion's immediate consequences for institutions' lending decisions. As previously discussed, most bank holding companies would not experience reductions in capital levels from the Tier 1 hybrid capital exclusion because the Dodd-Frank Act exempted existing hybrid instruments for most smaller institutions and gradually introduced the exclusions for the remaining institutions with $15 billion or more in assets. Also, institutions with more than $15 billion in assets generally have Tier 1 capital in excess of regulatory minimums, potentially further limiting their need for an immediate response to the hybrid capital exclusion.[34] Finally, institutions generally will be able to include excluded Tier 1 hybrid instruments in Tier 2 capital up to allowable limits, potentially minimizing effects on their total capital positions.[35]

Some institutions may still seek to maintain a target level of Tier 1 capital that exceeds regulatory minimums and is consistent with the level they had with Tier 1 hybrids. These institutions may prefer to maintain a capital buffer in excess of the minimum levels to satisfy regulators or investors and other market participants. In such cases, the institutions would experience a negative capital shock that could impact lending activity. To determine the potential impact of such an occurrence on lending activity, we designed a modified version of an established econometric model to estimate the effect of a change in Tier 1 capital levels on key credit market variables.[36] Specifically, we used the model to evaluate the dynamic responses of loan volume growth, lending spreads, and other important variables to temporary negative capital shocks representing the industry's potential responses to the hybrid capital exclusion. For example, if institutions wish to maintain the same Tier 1 leverage ratio, the capital deficit is the full difference between the capital ratios with and

---

[34]All bank holding companies with assets greater than $15 billion will continue to have Tier 1 risk-based capital and leverage ratios that exceed 6 percent and 4 percent, respectively, and therefore will meet the well-capitalized criteria we used in our analysis. A very small number of domestic subsidiaries of foreign banking institutions do not meet these standards, but the Federal Reserve generally has not required them to meet capital requirements. For more information on this policy, see GAO, *Bank Capital Requirements: Potential Effects of New Changes on Foreign Holding Companies and U.S. Banks Abroad*, GAO-12-160 (Washington, D.C.: Jan. 18, 2012).

[35]Bank holding companies face an overall limit on the amount of allowable Tier 2 capital equal to the amount of their Tier 1 capital.

[36]Specifically, the dynamic framework we use is known as a vector autoregression (VAR) methodology. Following Cara Lown and Donald P. Morgan, "The Credit Cycle and the Business Cycle: New Findings Using the Loan Officer Opinion Survey," *Journal of Money, Credit, and Banking*, vol. 38, (2006): 1575–97; and Jose M. Berrospide and Rochelle M. Edge, "'The Effects of Bank Capital on Lending: What Do We Know, and What Does It Mean?," *International Journal of Central Banking*, vol. 6 (December 2010), our model is a version of existing VAR models extended to include a banking sector. Our model includes four variables that capture supply, demand, output, and prices that comprise the "macroeconomy." We extend the model to include the credit market using various proxies for loan volumes, bank capital, loan spreads, and information on lending standards. The econometric approach has specific limitations but is considered a reasonable alternative to other types of models, including more sophisticated models. See appendix II for a fuller discussion of the methodology, assumptions, and limitations.

without the excluded Tier 1 hybrid instruments. Alternatively, institutions that are satisfied with a lower Tier 1 leverage ratio after the exclusions will have a smaller perceived capital deficit. As a result, we were able to analyze the impact under various assumptions about the institutions' collective desire to rebuild capital buffers.[37]

Although considerable uncertainty exists, our model suggests that the immediate effects of the Tier 1 hybrid exclusion on the cost and availability of credit likely will be modest. In the model, a negative capital shock related to implementation of the hybrid capital exclusion causes loan volumes to fall, lending standards to tighten, and lending spreads to rise. However, the implied shocks are relatively small, and the sensitivity of lending activity to changes in capital levels is moderate. Our results are generally consistent with other studies we identified in our review.[38] As table 5 shows, in the scenario in which institutions restore 100 percent of excluded hybrid capital to maintain consistent Tier 1 capital ratios, our model estimates an average 1.12 percentage point peak decline in loan growth between two quarters and a year after the exclusion goes into effect.[39] For lending spreads in this scenario, the model estimates an average 0.15 percentage point peak increase occurring about two to three quarters after the hybrid exclusion goes into effect. These effects on the cost and availability of credit are relatively modest and are even more so under less extreme scenarios that consider the amount of excluded hybrid capital that institutions replace.

---

[37]The hybrid capital exclusion results in a negative capital shock reducing the Tier 1 leverage ratio by around 1 percentage point at the aggregate level at most. Note that the negative shock to capital is designed to be temporary with all variables expected to return to normal levels over time. In general, the impulse response functions from the VAR system should return to zero if the system is stable.

[38]See appendix II for a complete list of studies we identified in our review.

[39]Estimates are based on impulse response functions from GAO's VAR model. The estimates assume an immediate negative shock to capital. The responses have very wide confidence intervals and should be interpreted with caution.

Table 5: Effects of Implied Capital Deficits on Loan Volumes and Lending Spreads for Institutions with More Than $15 Billion in Assets

	Capital shock scenario		
Implied replacement rate of hybrid instruments	Implied change in Tier 1 leverage ratio (percentage points)	Peak change in loan growth (percentage points)	Peak change in lending spreads (percentage points)
100%	-0.94	-1.12	0.15
70%	-0.66	-0.78	0.10
50%	-0.47	-0.56	0.07
25%	-0.23	-0.28	0.04
0%	0	0	0

Source: GAO analysis of Federal Reserve data.

Note: The model uses the Tier 1 leverage ratio for the capital target, although the Tier 1 risk-based ratio would produce generally similar results. "Implied replacement rate of hybrid instruments" refers to actions institutions take to restore their Tier 1 capital ratio to the level that would be equivalent to the direct replacement of the hybrid instruments. Impact estimates are based on impulse response function from GAO's VAR model. The estimates assume an immediate negative shock with no transition period. The effects of the shock to capital are traced out of 12 quarters that by design return to zero. Estimates in the table represent the peak effects based on two different modeling specifications. See appendix II for further information.

Our results assume that banking institutions immediately address capital reductions resulting from Tier 1 hybrid exclusions. Given that these institutions would continue to meet minimum capital requirements and expect the change to the use of Tier 1 hybrid capital, they are more likely to replace—if they elected to do so—any hybrid instruments slowly over a number of years. The Dodd-Frank Act excludes existing Tier 1 hybrid instruments over 3 years beginning in 2013 (for institutions with more than $15 billion in assets), also implying more limited effects on lending activity.

However, the immediate effects on overall lending activity may be more significant for certain loan types. For example, the hybrid capital exclusion could affect volumes of commercial and industrial loans more significantly than other types of loans because markets for these loans appear more sensitive to changes in bank capital. The peak decline in loan growth from a negative capital shock is roughly 2.26 percentage points for commercial and industrial loans or about two times larger than the impact suggested for aggregate loan volumes (1.12 percentage points). Other studies also have found that commercial and industrial loans are more strongly affected by capital ratios than other types of loans.[40] Moreover, the model parameters are aggregate estimates and may not generalize to the specific circumstances of some banks. For example, our model suggests that banks will adjust lending spreads and loan volumes in response to the hybrid restriction. However some banks may not be able to raise rates and would likely have to take other actions, including reducing loan volumes by more than is suggested here.

Although other studies found similar results, our estimates generally should be interpreted with caution, given the methodological and other limitations inherent in this type of analysis. For example, many of the specific estimates are not statistically significant with respect to the actual size of the hybrid capital exclusion's effects, if any—meaning that they are not statistically different from zero.[41] Given the limitations, we compared the results of our model to a wider body of empirical literature.[42] In general, these sources also found small to moderate effects on lending activity from changes to bank capital.[43]

Applying estimates of the impact of capital on lending activity from available studies to the potential deficit created by the hybrid capital

---

[40]See, for example, Diana Hancock, Andrew J. Laing, and James A. Wilcox, "Bank Capital Shocks: Dynamic Effects on Securities, Loans, and Capital," *Journal of Banking and Finance* (1995): 661-77.

[41]For example, our estimates have wide confidence intervals suggesting considerable uncertainty in the results (see app. II for limitations).

[42]See, for example, Berrospide and Edge, "The Effects of Bank Capital"; Mark A. Carlson, Hui Shan, and Missaka Warusawitharana, "Capital Ratios and Bank Lending: A Matched Bank Approach," Federal Reserve Board working paper No. 2011-34 (July 1, 2011); and Thomas Cosimano and Dalia Hakura, "Bank Behavior in Response to Basel III: A Cross-Country Analysis," IMF working paper No. 11/119 (Washington, D.C., 2011).

[43]Responses to the Federal Reserve's *Senior Loan Officer Opinion Survey* suggest that deterioration in banks' capital positions ranked as the least important reason behind banks decision to tighten lending standards during the most recent financial crisis. See Berrospide and Edge (2010).

exclusion results in a range of effects.[44] For example, when we assume that institutions target capital ratios equivalent to replacing 70 percent of excluded hybrid instruments, estimates range from a decline of 0.13 to 1.81 percentage points for loan volumes and from an increase of 0.06 to 0.43 percentage points for lending spreads. Although exact comparisons are not always possible, the averages of the estimates are generally consistent with our model results.[45] Like our own analysis, some of the studies examine the impact of a generalized shock to capital. However, in the case of the Tier 1 hybrid capital exclusion, the capital shock is specific to bank holding companies with assets of $15 billion or more. Given the large number of banking institutions with assets of less than $15 billion, the ability of affected institutions to raise loan rates significantly may be limited by competitive forces, and the decline in loan growth may be mitigated by substitution across institutions.

Long-Term Effects of Raising Tier 1 Capital without Less Costly Hybrid Instruments

Long-term effects of the hybrid capital exclusion on loan rates will likely also be small, although the exact impact is unknown. Without Tier 1 hybrid instruments, loan rates could increase if capital costs rise for institutions that have relied on these instruments as a cheaper source of regulatory capital. To assess the potential impact on loan rates for these institutions, we used a modified version of an existing loan pricing model.[46] Banking institutions have multiple options for adjusting to more costly forms of Tier 1 capital—such as shifting lending activity to lower-risk borrowers, reducing returns to shareholders, increasing efficiency, or raising lending rates—and the loan pricing model allowed us to consider

---

[44]The studies included in these estimates are reported in appendix II. Each study allowed us to determine the impact of a 1 percentage point change in capital on loan volumes and lending rates. (For example, our model implies that a 1 percentage point shock to capital results in a decline in aggregate loan growth of 1.2 percentage points and an increase in lending spreads of roughly 0.16 percentage points.) We then scaled the estimates by the size of the expected capital deficit as a result of the hybrid restriction. Because most of the other studies are focused on specific episodes of credit contraction or on Basel III, they make different assumptions that make strict comparisons difficult, including about the time period over which the impact is measured.

[45]For example some studies look at peak effects, while others examine long-run effects. These studies represent a variety of different methodologies ranging from regression techniques to large-scale macroeconomic and general equilbrium models, each with its own limitations. General equilibrium models attempt to model various aspects of the economy when bank balance sheets and credit markets can be modeled explicitly and allow for consistent counterfactual experiments with different policy scenarios.

[46]For information on our model and the model we modified, see appendix II.

these different scenarios. For all of the scenarios we examined, our model indicated minimal potential loan rate increases from institutions' use of higher cost and quality Tier 1 capital and, as a result, modest effects on loan volumes (table 6). Even if institutions are assumed to adjust solely by raising lending rates, rates would increase by 0.12 percentage points. Other scenarios assuming that institutions' adjustments also occurred in other areas led to smaller increases in lending rates. The long-term effects on lending rates may be more significant for certain institutions. For example, customers of smaller institutions could experience larger increases in loan rates, but even these effects likely will remain modest.[47] Again, the effects on lending rates would likely be mitigated since it may be difficult for the impacted institutions to pass the higher cost on to borrowers without losing market share.

Table 6: Estimates of Tier 1 Hybrid Exclusion on Loan Rates under Different Illustrative Scenarios

Key values	Starting values	Scenario 1[a]	Scenario 2[b]	Scenario 3[c]	Scenario 4[d]
All banking institutions					
Loan rate	5.59%	5.71%	5.61%	5.61%	5.63%
Return on equity	15.00%	15.00%	14.75%	15.00%	15.00%
Yield on debt	2.57%	2.57%	2.55%	2.57%	2.57%
Credit spread	1.05%	1.05%	1.05%	1.00%	1.05%
Administrative costs	1.03%	1.03%	1.03%	1.03%	1.00%
Increase in loan rate (percentage points)		0.12	0.03	0.02	0.04
Smaller banking institutions[e]					
Loan rate	6.61%	6.82%	6.68%	6.67%	6.69%
Return on equity	15.00%	15.00%	14.80%	15.00%	15.00%
Yield on debt	3.38%	3.38%	3.36%	3.38%	3.38%
Credit spread	0.90%	0.90%	0.90%	0.85%	0.90%
Administrative costs	1.32%	1.32%	1.32%	1.32%	1.29%
Increase in loan rate (percentage points)		0.21	0.07	0.06	0.08

Sources: GAO and The Brookings Institution.

---

[47]For the illustrative purposes of our model, we defined smaller institutions as those with between $1 billion and $10 billion in total assets.

GAO-12-237 Hybrid Capital Instruments

Notes: The Brookings Institution sources are Douglas J. Elliott, "Quantifying the Effects on Lending of Increased Capital Requirements," Brookings briefing paper (Washington, D.C., 2009); and Douglas J. Elliott, "A Further Exploration of Bank Capital Requirements: Effects of Competition from Other Financial Sectors and Effects of Size of Bank or Borrower and Loan Types," Brookings briefing paper (Washington, D.C., 2010).

Scenarios are based on a loan pricing equation in which the loan rate equals the weighted cost of capital. We assumed that the yield on hybrids reflects the yield on trust preferred securities, which is assumed to be slightly higher for small banking institutions. The actual cost of trust preferred securities and noncumulative perpetual preferred securities will vary according to the issuing institution and market conditions. See appendix II for details, assumptions, and limitations.

[a]Scenario 1 illustrates the effects of banking institutions adjusting to the hybrid exclusion solely by raising loan rates to increase their retained earnings.

[b]Scenario 2 illustrates the effects of banking institutions raising rates but also having investors view the institution as less risky. We assume that the return on equity decreases by 0.25 percentage points and that the yield on debt decreases by 0.02 percentage points.

[c]Scenario 3 illustrates the effects of banking institutions raising rates and also shifting their lending activity toward loans with less risk. By reducing the amount of risk, we assume that the credit spread of the institutions' assets, which is equal to the probability-weighted expected loss, declines by 0.05 percentage points.

[d]Scenario 4 illustrates the effects of banking institutions raising rates and also taking steps to lower administrative cost associated with loans by 0.03 percentage points.

[e]For the illustrative purposes of our model, we defined smaller institutions as those with between $1 billion and $10 billion in total assets.

Some U.S. Institutions May Face a Tax Disadvantage Relative to Foreign Peers

The lack of tax-deductible Tier 1 hybrid capital instruments could result in a cost disadvantage for U.S. institutions relative to their foreign peers, although the overall competitive effects are unclear.[48] Hybrid capital instruments, in particular trust preferred securities and real estate investment trust (REIT) preferred securities, generally have been the primary Tier 1 capital instruments for which U.S. institutions have received tax-deductible treatment.[49] In the United States, debt instruments receive favorable tax treatment compared to equity. The tax code generally allows interest expenses on debt instruments to be deducted from income, but not dividends or other payments to equity

---

[48]For the purposes of this section, hybrid generally refers to capital instruments other than common equity rather than to the specific instruments that the Federal Reserve classifies as restricted core capital elements.

[49]REIT preferred securities are noncumulative preferred shares issued by a special-purpose entity established by a bank as a wholly owned subsidiary that qualifies for REIT tax status. The REIT uses proceeds from the sale of the preferred shares to purchase qualifying real estate assets from its parent bank and pays dividends on the preferred shares using income from the real estate assets. A bank can deduct from its income dividends paid by its REIT subsidiary as long as the REIT complies with federal income tax rules.

holders. According to market participants, other Tier 1 capital instruments such as preferred stock generally have not qualified for tax advantages because their equitylike features, such as a perpetual maturity or noncumulative dividends, disqualify them from IRS consideration as debt instruments. Market participants said that a favorable tax treatment is one of the primary reasons banking institutions use hybrid capital. In addition, the Federal Reserve has identified the importance of trust preferred securities' tax advantages to the competitiveness of U.S. banking institutions as a reason for allowing the instruments as Tier 1 capital.

Changes to the definition of Tier 1 capital resulting from the Dodd-Frank Act and Basel III effectively eliminate hybrid capital instruments that qualify for tax-deductible status in the United States. Both the Dodd-Frank Act and Basel III prevent the use of trust preferred securities in Tier 1 capital, and Basel III restricts the use of REIT preferred securities for large banking institutions. In addition to the Dodd-Frank Act's exclusion of trust preferred securities, Basel III contains provisions that would eliminate the instruments' use as Tier 1 capital, although over a longer period.[50] The Basel III framework requires Tier 1 instruments that are not common equity to meet certain criteria—including having a perpetual maturity and discretionary, noncumulative dividends—that effectively exclude trust preferred securities. Furthermore, Basel III limits the amount of Tier 1 capital credit for instruments such as REIT preferred, hindering their use as a tax-advantaged source of Tier 1 capital, according to market participants. The Basel III standards provide a single global definition of bank regulatory capital, but how those standards are adopted and implemented depends on statutory and regulatory action by national authorities.[51] To promote complete and globally consistent implementation, the Basel Committee established a framework to monitor and review implementation of Basel III capital requirements.

However, some foreign jurisdictions have tax codes that may allow tax advantages for hybrid instruments that would still qualify as Tier 1 under

---

[50]The Dodd-Frank Act allows institutions with less than $15 billion in total assets to continue including existing hybrid instruments in Tier 1 and phases out Tier 1 treatment of such instruments for institutions over $15 billion from 2013 through 2016. Basel III phases out Tier 1 treatment of hybrid (noncommon equity) Tier 1 instruments for all internationally active banking institutions from 2013 through 2022.

[51]Basel III requires member countries to complete implementation by translating the rules into national laws and regulations prior to January 1, 2013.

the new Basel III definition, potentially leaving U.S. institutions with a cost-of-capital disadvantage. The tax treatment of capital instruments—such as the ability to deduct interest or dividend payments—differs across countries based on their domestic tax regimes, potentially resulting in varied after-tax costs of Tier 1 instruments across countries. According to market participants, some foreign jurisdictions—particularly in Europe—allow tax deductibility of some perpetual, noncumulative capital instruments that would still meet Basel III Tier 1 criteria. For example, a 2006 report by the Committee of European Bank Supervisors indicated that European countries such as France, Germany, Spain, and the United Kingdom allow tax deductibility of some types of noncumulative, perpetual instruments that are not tax deductible in the United States.[52] In a 2007 report on the use of hybrid capital instruments in Europe, the same organization found that almost all Tier 1 hybrid instruments in Europe were perpetual (95 percent) and noncumulative (93 percent).[53] Market participants indicated that the lack of tax-deductible Tier 1 capital could result in a cost of capital disadvantage for U.S. institutions relative to their international peers. The longer time frame for excluding trust preferred securities and other Tier 1 hybrid instruments under Basel III rules also could present a cost-of-capital disadvantage for U.S. banking institutions during the extended phase-out period.

The international competitive effects of any such disadvantage for U.S. institutions are uncertain given the scope and significance of other regulatory reforms occurring domestically and globally. Basel III and the Dodd-Frank Act include many significant changes to capital requirements and financial regulation that may have consequences for the international competitiveness of U.S. banking institutions—consequences that are equal to or greater than the consequences of the changes to Tier 1 hybrid

---

[52]Committee of European Banking Supervisors, *Survey of the Implementation of the Current Rules on Own Funds Across Member States: Annex 8—Overview of Hybrid Instruments Eligible as Original Own Funds* (London, UK: June 23, 2006).

[53]Committee of European Banking Supervisors, *Report on a Quantitative Analysis of the Characteristics of Hybrids in the European Economic Area* (London, UK: Mar. 13, 2007). The definition of Tier 1 hybrid instruments used by the Committee of European Bank Supervisors differs from the definition used in our report, which is based on the Federal Reserve's restricted core capital elements and does not include noncumulative preferred stock. The Committee of European Bank Supervisors uses a broader definition that includes (1) innovative instruments with an incentive to redeem such as step-up features; (2) noninnovative instruments that do not have incentives to redeem, and (3) noncumulative perpetual preference shares.

capital rules. For example, Basel III increases required capital levels; introduces additional capital buffers; expands its coverage of risks, including those from securitizations and trading counterparties; and introduces a leverage ratio requirement and liquidity standards. The Dodd-Frank Act introduced fundamental reforms across the banking and financial regulatory systems, including changes to the regulation of systemic risks, the trading and investment activities of banking institutions, the use and trading of derivatives, securities regulation, and the structure of bank supervision. The extent to which these regulatory reforms may interact to present additional competitive advantages or disadvantages to U.S. banking institutions relative to their foreign peers will determine the ultimate significance of any tax disadvantage from hybrid instruments.

In addition, market participants identified other factors that might affect any international competitiveness implications of not permitting tax-deductible Tier 1 hybrid instruments. First, U.S. regulators have not yet proposed rules for implementing Basel III, and their decisions on how, when, and for which institutions the provisions will apply may limit potential tax disadvantages. For example, one banking institution said that U.S. regulators could choose not to apply Basel III minority interest deductions to REIT preferred securities because regulators can require that the instruments be converted to preferred shares when necessary to absorb financial losses more effectively. Second, concerns about a cost-of-capital disadvantage would apply only to the largest U.S. banks that compete globally rather than to the many smaller banking institutions that compete with each other domestically. Third, institutions in some foreign jurisdictions may face competitive disadvantages from a more stringent application of Basel III rules for hybrid instruments. For example, European authorities said that draft rules for European institutions require an explicit loss absorption mechanism—such as the ability to write down or convert the hybrid instrument to equity—for all Tier 1 hybrid instruments, while the Basel III rules require such features only for some instruments (not including preferred shares). Finally, hybrid instruments will have a more limited role than in the past because of increased regulatory requirements for the amount of common equity in Tier 1, potentially moderating any competitive disadvantages from differences in the cost of Tier 1 hybrid capital. For example, the common equity requirement under Basel III represents over 80 percent of the overall Tier 1 capital requirement, and the share is higher for systemically important institutions.[54] A higher requirement for common equity results in a smaller scope for using hybrid instruments to meet overall Tier 1 levels. Previous Basel guidelines called for common equity to make up only the predominant share of overall Tier 1—effectively 51 percent.[55] Thus, any cost of capital disadvantages from Tier 1 hybrid instruments may be relatively less significant than under prior international regulatory capital frameworks.

Smaller Banking Institutions Face Limited Capital-Raising Options but Report Little Unmet Capital Need

Smaller banking institutions generally had limited options for raising capital, and one important form of capital—trust preferred securities—is now largely unavailable to these banks.[56] According to market participants we interviewed, around 2000 or earlier, smaller institutions had little to no access to public capital markets, in part because their offerings were not large enough to attract investors. Starting in 2000, investment banks began pooling the trust preferred securities of many smaller institutions and selling shares of those pools to investors. This pooling of trust preferred securities expanded smaller institutions' access to capital by removing many of the previous obstacles to attracting investors. For example, the pooled structures received combined credit ratings for all of the underlying issuers, while many smaller institutions did not receive individual ratings. As a result, for the first time, smaller institutions were able to access significant amounts of capital from investors who required credit ratings.

Trust preferred securities quickly became a popular option for smaller institutions to access capital. Available data show that, from 2000 to 2007, trust preferred securities accounted for over half of all regulatory capital offerings made by smaller institutions and totaled more than $23

---

[54]Basel III requires systemically important banking institutions to meet a minimum additional Tier 1 capital requirement comprised entirely of common equity and ranging from 1 percent to 2.5 percent depending on the institution's systemic importance.

[55]Basel Committee on Banking Supervision press release, "Instruments eligible for inclusion in Tier 1 capital" (Oct. 27, 1998).

[56]Smaller banking institutions are defined as banks, thrifts, and bank and thrift holding companies with less than $10 billion in total assets. For the purposes of this section, capital generally refers to capital instruments that an institution's primary federal regulator has permitted as Tier 1 or Tier 2 regulatory capital.

billion (see fig. 8).[57] Based on our nationally representative survey, we estimate that 30 percent of smaller institutions considered that prior to January 1, 2008, their ability to issue trust preferred securities (including pools of trust preferred securities) had been beneficial to their ability to access regulatory capital.[58] About half of institutions did not issue any trust preferred securities, and 10 percent considered their ability to issue trust preferred securities not at all beneficial.[59]

---

[57] These data include offerings of capital instruments that may be counted as Tier 1 or Tier 2 regulatory capital: common stock, preferred stock, trust preferred securities, and subordinated debt. These data are from SNL Financial, which obtains information on capital offerings from SEC filings and press releases. While these data include public and private offerings, they do not reflect capital raises by institutions that do not file with SEC, do not have parent companies that file with SEC, and are not publicly traded, such as some small institutions that may receive equity investments from board members or the local community. Comprehensive data on private capital raises were unavailable.

[58] GAO conducted a nationwide representative web-based survey of banks, thrifts, and holding companies with less than $10 billion in total assets from June to August 2011. We received valid responses from 510 (64 percent) out of the 794 sampled banking institutions. The weighted response rate was 66 percent. All percentage estimates have a 95 percent confidence level of ± 7 percentage points or less. This estimate represents those respondents who answered either "greatly beneficial" or "moderately beneficial" to the survey question. For more details on the survey methodology and questions, see appendixes I and III.

[59] The remaining respondents reported "no opinion."

Figure 8: Smaller Banking Institutions' Capital Offerings, 2000-2011

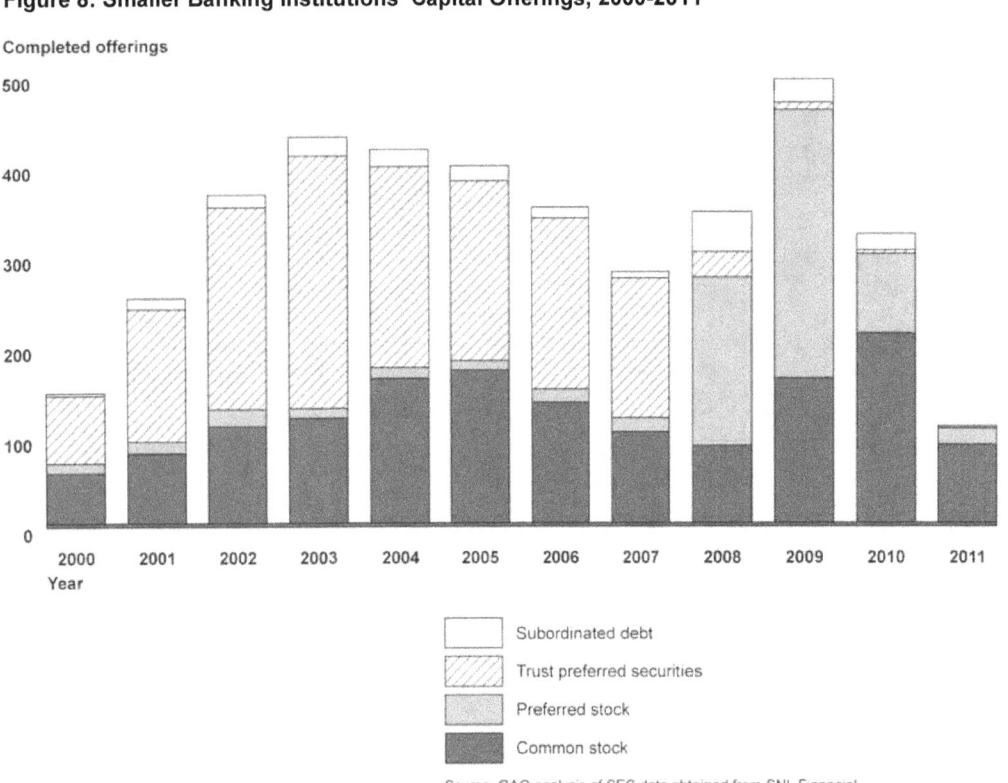

Completed offerings

Legend:
- Subordinated debt
- Trust preferred securities
- Preferred stock
- Common stock

Source: GAO analysis of SEC data obtained from SNL Financial.

Note: Figures for 2011 represent only the first two quarters.

During and following the financial crisis, however, offerings of trust preferred securities dropped considerably. According to market participants, investors were no longer interested in purchasing trust preferred securities, partly because of their performance during the financial crisis and concerns about new regulatory restrictions such as those under the Dodd-Frank Act. Specifically, many investors in trust preferred securities found that the instruments did not meet their expectations during the crisis. For example, more institutions deferred dividends than investors had expected, particularly smaller institutions. Additionally, pools of trust preferred securities did not prove to be as diversified as anticipated. After 2007, trust preferred securities accounted for a much smaller share of smaller institutions' regulatory capital offerings—just 3 percent from 2008 through 2010—and no smaller institutions offered trust preferred securities in the first half of 2011. Based on our survey, an estimated 12 percent of smaller institutions would likely be able to raise trust preferred securities within the next year.[60]

With trust preferred securities largely unavailable, smaller institutions increased their reliance on other types of preferred shares as a capital source, largely through investments from the Treasury Department's Troubled Asset Relief Program (TARP). Prior to the financial crisis, smaller banking institutions rarely issued preferred shares that were not pooled into trust preferred securities. For example, between 2000 and 2007, preferred shares accounted for 4 percent of the number of regulatory capital offerings of smaller institutions. However, in 2008 and 2009, when TARP made its investments in hundreds of banking institutions, over half (58 percent) of smaller institutions' capital offerings were in the form of preferred shares. Of these, 82 percent were offered through TARP. As the federal government is no longer making new capital investments in banking institutions, smaller institutions will likely face more limited access to preferred shares in the future. For example, preferred shares accounted for only 17 percent of smaller institutions' capital offerings in the first half of 2011.

Common equity now predominates, and the most available source of capital for smaller institutions is equity investments from board members or the local community. In 2010 and 2011, most capital offerings by smaller institutions (70 percent) were in the form of common equity. In 2010, smaller institutions raised more common equity—$7 billion—than in any year between 2000 and 2009, a period when the average amount raised annually was $3.4 billion. Based on our survey results, we estimate that 70 percent of smaller institutions would likely be able to raise equity capital from board members or their local community within the next year. However, smaller institutions were considerably less likely to be able to raise capital in other forms during this time. For example, we estimate that about 30 percent of institutions would likely be able to raise preferred equity from a private placement, subordinated debt, or common equity from a public offering, and the estimated percentages are lower for preferred equity from a public offering and trust preferred securities (see fig. 9).

---

[60]The percentage estimates of smaller institutions that would likely be able to raise capital reflect the "very likely" and "somewhat likely" responses to the survey question.

Figure 9: Perceived Ability of Smaller Institutions to Successfully Raise Capital, as of August 15, 2011

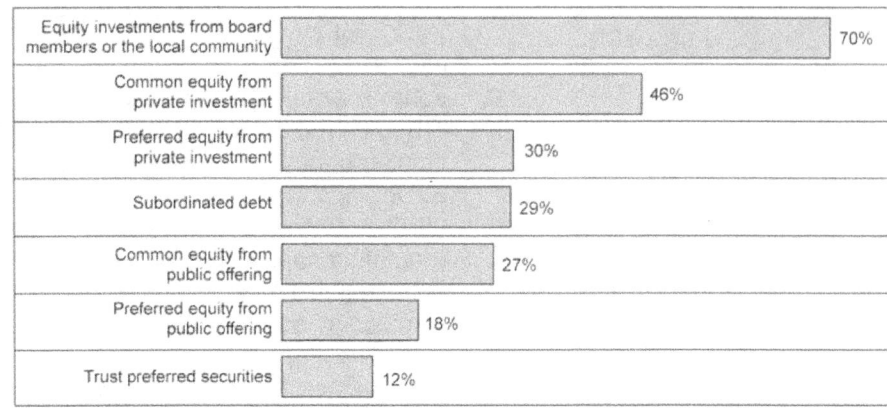

Equity investments from board members or the local community	70%
Common equity from private investment	46%
Preferred equity from private investment	30%
Subordinated debt	29%
Common equity from public offering	27%
Preferred equity from public offering	18%
Trust preferred securities	12%

Source: GAO survey of smaller banking institutions.

Notes: Estimates reflect "very likely" and "somewhat likely" responses to the survey question "How likely is it that your institution would be able to raise the following types of regulatory capital at acceptable cost, terms, and conditions within the next year?"

Percentages are estimates based on the results of our nationally representative sample of smaller banking institutions. All estimates have a margin of error of less than 7 percentage points.

Smaller Institutions' Ability to Raise Capital Varies by Financial Condition and Other Factors

Smaller institutions consider their financial condition and performance (for example, profitability, debt and capital levels, and asset quality) as the most important factor in their ability to successfully access capital. Based on our survey results, we estimate that 87 percent of smaller institutions consider financial condition and performance as a very important factor in their ability to raise capital. Market participants noted that investors may be concerned about smaller institutions' loan portfolios and concentrations in commercial real estate. They explained that smaller institutions tend to have greater geographic concentration and fewer business lines and tend also to focus on traditional lending, which has not been profitable recently. Management quality was the second most important factor, with 74 percent considering it as very important to raising capital. One smaller institution with less than $100 million in total assets noted that it could raise capital fairly easily from existing investors and local customers but added that they would have to perceive the bank's performance and management as satisfactory. Smaller institutions rated several other factors as important to their ability to successfully raise capital, including growth potential, the economic environment in their lending area, and familiarity with investors.

Additionally, results from our survey showed that smaller banking institutions' ability to raise different forms of capital varied somewhat by factors such as asset size, ownership type (public or private), institution type (bank or thrift), and organization structure (holding company or stand-alone). For example, we estimate that a larger proportion of public institutions and institutions with total assets of between $500 million and $10 billion were likely to be able to raise common equity from a private capital offering than were private institutions and institutions with less than $500 million in total assets. Also, a larger proportion of banks and holding companies were likely to be able to raise subordinated debt than were thrifts and stand-alone institutions without a holding company. However, most of these groups saw equity investments from board members or the local community as the most available form of capital.

The current regulatory capital-raising environment was described as very challenging for an estimated 44 percent of smaller banking institutions and moderately challenging for an additional 32 percent, for several reasons. Smaller institutions most often considered the economic climate and laws and regulations as challenges to their institutions' ability to raise capital. Specifically, 89 percent of smaller institutions found the economic climate, market conditions, or both to be challenging to their ability to raise capital, and 86 percent found laws and regulations to be challenging.[61] Several respondents identified SEC rules that apply additional reporting requirements to institutions exceeding 500 shareholders as a constraint on their ability to raise capital from new investors.[62] Other factors that the majority of smaller institutions identified as challenging included the transaction costs of conducting a public offering, lack of access to public capital markets, and investors' preference for large offerings.

---

[61]The percentage estimates of smaller institutions that considered certain factors as challenging reflect the "very challenging" and "moderately challenging" response options to the survey question.

[62]Under Securities Exchange Act Section 12(g), an issuer with 500 or more holders of a class of its equity securities and assets in excess of $10 million generally must register that class of security with the Securities and Exchange Commission. See 15 U.S.C. § 78l(g)(1)(B); 17 C.F.R. § 240.12g-1.

Market participants also identified several factors that inhibited smaller institutions' access to public capital markets. For example, some investors have minimum investment requirements and cannot make investments below a certain size. At the same time, limitations on the share of ownership of banks—beyond which investors would have to register as a bank holding company—restrict the share of equity securities that most investors are willing to purchase. According to some market participants, the minimum investment size requirements, along with ownership limitations, eliminate many investors as a potential capital source for small institutions. Additionally, market participants said that potential investors generally were not willing to devote resources to researching offerings of relatively small banks because the research required for a small offering was nearly the same as it would be for a larger offering that would provide more potential for a higher absolute return. Also, market participants noted that investors generally required that the securities they purchased be liquid—that is, easily resold at a reasonable price. The capital offerings of smaller institutions typically have less liquidity than those of larger institutions because a more limited group of investors is able and willing to purchase the instruments, and they are traded less frequently. Finally, market participants reported that credit rating agencies generally did not rate the offerings of smaller institutions, which can restrict access to public capital markets.

A Majority of Smaller Institutions Report No Unmet Capital Need

Most smaller institutions have not raised capital since January 1, 2008, and the majority of those reported no need for or interest in additional capital (see fig. 10). Specifically, we estimate that 65 percent of smaller institutions have not raised capital since January 1, 2008, and 88 percent of those did not need or want to raise more regulatory capital. Only 3 percent of smaller institutions that had not raised capital since January 1, 2008, attempted to raise capital but were unable to do so.

Figure 10: Capital-Raising Activity among Smaller Institutions since January 1, 2008, as of August 15, 2011

Smaller institutions that have raised capital since 2008

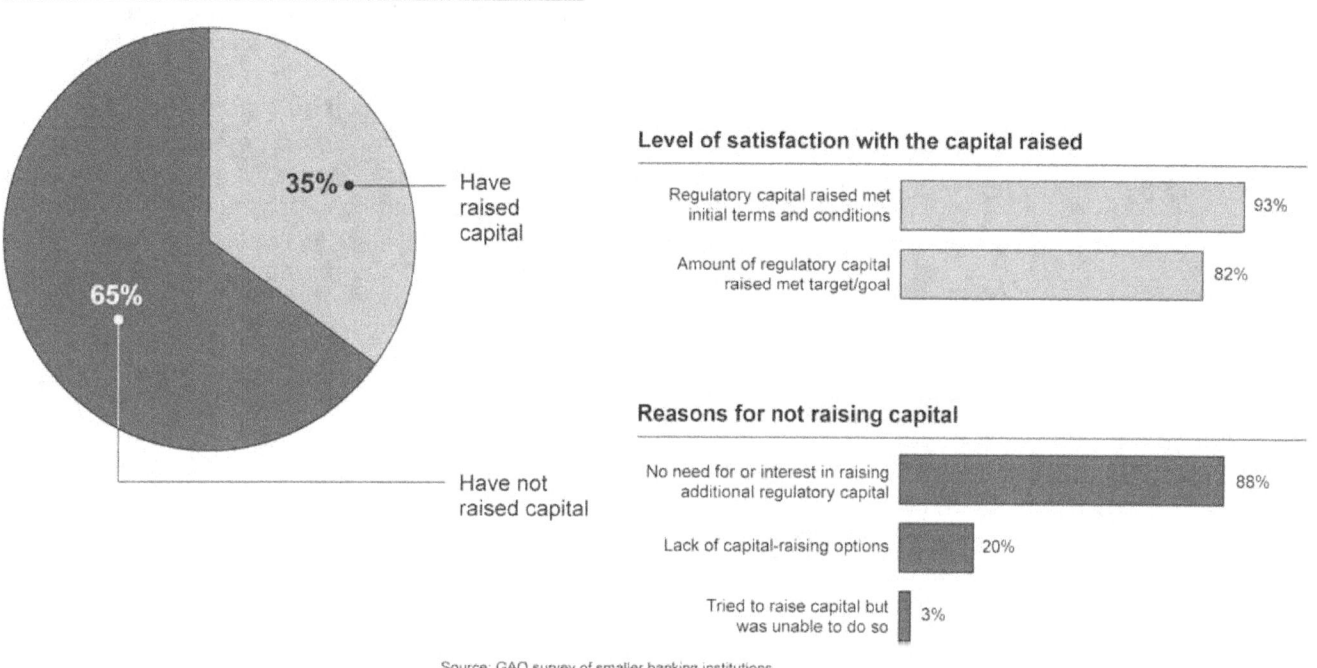

Source: GAO survey of smaller banking institutions.

Note: Percentages are estimates based on the results of our nationally representative sample of smaller banking institutions. All estimates have a margin of error of less than 7 percentage points.

The smaller institutions that had raised capital since January 1, 2008, were generally satisfied with the capital they had raised. We estimate that 35 percent of smaller institutions had raised regulatory capital since January 1, 2008. Of these institutions, 82 percent reported that the amount of regulatory capital raised met their goal, and 93 percent reported that it met their initial terms and conditions.

Institutions whose financial condition was relatively strong generally had a more favorable view of the capital-raising environment. Supervisory examination ratings assigned by a banking institution's primary regulator generally assess the institutions' financial condition and performance.[63] According to our survey results, institutions that found the current regulatory capital-raising environment challenging had weaker supervisory ratings on average than institutions that did not find the environment challenging (see fig. 11). Furthermore, among smaller institutions that raised capital, the institutions that met their initial targets had significantly stronger supervisory ratings than institutions that did not meet their target amounts. Consistent with our survey results, market participants noted that capital was available for relatively healthy institutions that sought capital to support growth opportunities but was largely unavailable to weaker institutions seeking capital to address problems with their financial condition and performance.

---

[63]The federal banking agencies assign a supervisory rating when they conduct examinations of a bank or thrift's safety and soundness. The numerical ratings range from 1 to 5, with 1 being the strongest and 5 the weakest. The ratings—referred to as CAMELS—assess six components of an institution's financial health: capital, asset quality, management, earnings, liquidity, and sensitivity to market risk. The Federal Reserve also uses ratings to measure the overall condition of bank and thrift holding companies.

Figure 11: Smaller Institutions' Views of the Capital-Raising Environment by Supervisory Rating, as of August 15, 2011

Institutions that found the capital-raising environment challenging

Institutions that did not find the capital-raising environment challenging

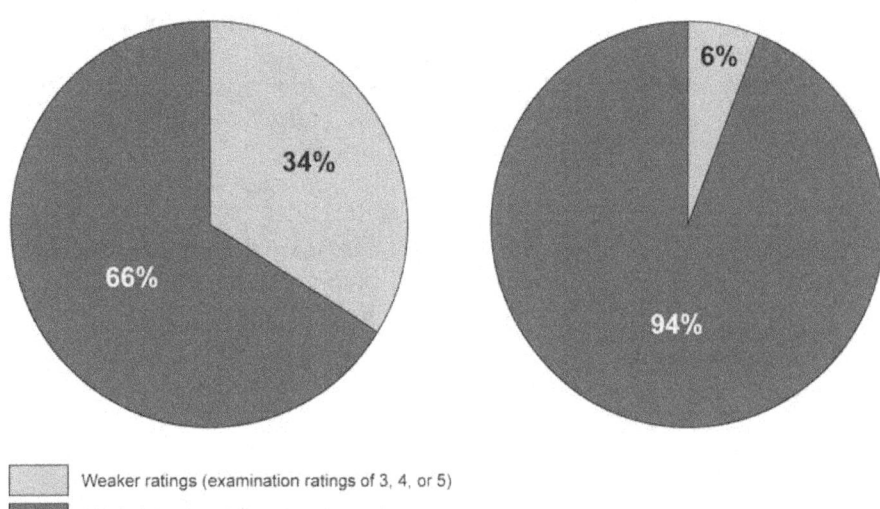

Weaker ratings (examination ratings of 3, 4, or 5)

Stronger ratings (examination ratings of 1 or 2)

Source: GAO survey of smaller banking institutions and FDIC, Federal Reserve, and OTS supervisory examination ratings.

Note: Percentages are estimates based on the results of our nationally representative sample of smaller banking institutions. All estimates have a margin of error of less than 7 percentage points.

Agency Comments

We provided a draft of this report to FDIC, the Federal Reserve, and OCC for their review and comment. FDIC and the Federal Reserve provided technical comments that were incorporated, as appropriate.

We are sending copies of this report to appropriate congressional committees, FDIC, the Federal Reserve, OCC, and other interested parties. In addition, the report is available at no charge on the GAO website at http://www.gao.gov.

If you or your staff have any questions about this report, please contact me at (202) 512-2642 or mccoolt@gao.gov. Contact points for our Offices of Congressional Relations and Public Affairs may be found on the last page of this report. GAO staff who made key contributions to this report are listed in appendix IV.

Thomas J. McCool
Director
Center for Economics,
Applied Research and Methods

Appendix I: Objectives, Scope, and Methodology

The objectives of our report were to examine (1) the use of hybrid capital instruments as Tier 1 capital and the benefits and risks of including them in this category, (2) the potential effects on banking institutions and the economy of prohibiting the use of hybrid instruments to meet Tier 1 capital requirements, and (3) options that exist for smaller banking institutions to access regulatory capital.

Use of Tier 1 Hybrid Capital Instruments and Their Benefits and Risks

To describe the use of Tier 1 hybrid capital instruments, we analyzed data from banking institutions' regulatory financial filings and reviewed relevant federal banking regulations. To determine the instruments that were eligible for Tier 1 capital treatment for various banking institutions, we reviewed the statutes and regulations concerning capital requirements for banks (including national banks, state member banks, and state nonmember banks), thrifts, and bank and thrift holding companies. We also interviewed federal banking regulators—specifically, from the Federal Deposit Insurance Corporation (FDIC), the Board of Governors of the Federal Reserve System (Federal Reserve), the Office of the Comptroller of the Currency (OCC), and the Office of Thrift Supervision (OTS)—to determine the regulatory treatment of hybrid capital instruments for different banking institutions. We defined the scope of this report to focus on instruments that the Federal Reserve made eligible for limited inclusion in Tier 1 capital for bank holding companies but were not allowed for other types of banking institutions. These instruments—defined by the Federal Reserve as restricted core capital elements—will be excluded from Tier 1 capital by the Dodd-Frank Wall Street Reform and Consumer Protection Act (Dodd-Frank Act) and include trust preferred securities, which are widely recognized as the most common hybrid capital instrument. Because federal banking regulators did not allow these instruments as Tier 1 capital for depository institutions—banks and thrifts—our review focused on the use of hybrid instruments by holding companies.

To assess the use of hybrid instruments by bank holding companies, we analyzed data that these institutions report to the Federal Reserve annually on form FR Y-9C, "Consolidated Financial Statements for Bank Holding Companies." This report is filed by all top-level bank holding companies with $500 million or more in consolidated total assets and by select institutions with less than $500 million in total assets. The Federal Reserve supervises approximately 5,000 top-level bank holding companies, although most of these do not file form FR Y-9C and are not subject to Tier 1 capital requirements because of their small asset size. For December 31, 2010, our data included 969 top-level bank holding

companies. We removed a small number of institutions from our data that
reported "NA" for total assets. We also removed a small number of
domestic subsidiaries of foreign banking institutions that the Federal
Reserve exempted from Tier 1 capital requirements. We analyzed year-
end data from 1997—the first full year following the Federal Reserve's
decision to allow trust preferred securities as Tier 1 capital—through
2010, the most recent year with complete data available. We collected the
FR Y-9C data using SNL Financial, a private data provider, and
calculated the amount of hybrid instruments eligible for inclusion in Tier 1
in consultation with the Federal Reserve.

We also assessed the use of hybrid capital instruments by thrift holding
companies. Although thrift holding companies were not subject to uniform
Tier 1 capital requirements, they were informally assessed under rules
similar to the Federal Reserve's rules for bank holding companies,
according to OTS officials.[1] As such, we included thrift holding companies
in our analysis using a proxy Tier 1 calculation described in the OTS
examiner's handbook for thrift holding companies. We obtained data on
thrift holding companies from the holding company schedule in the Thrift
Financial Report filed by OTS-supervised institutions. The data included
some institutions that were not top-level consolidated thrift holding
companies, and we removed them from our analysis after discussions
with a former OTS official who is now at FDIC.[2] We used SNL Financial
and the Federal Reserve's National Information Center to determine
which records to remove from our analysis. Because data from the Thrift
Financial Report includes fewer fields than the FR Y-9C, we limited our
analysis to thrift holding companies' use of trust preferred securities from
year-end 2004 to year-end 2010. Data on thrift holding companies' use of
trust preferred securities was not available prior to 2004.

To describe the benefits and risks of including hybrid instruments as Tier
1 capital, we collected and reviewed studies and other documentary
evidence from federal regulators, industry participants and observers, and
academic sources. We conducted interviews with market participants,

---

[1]As a result of the Dodd-Frank Act, thrift holding companies will be subject to uniform
capital requirements in the future and will face the same restrictions on hybrid capital as
bank holding companies.

[2]Most OTS staff were reassigned to other federal banking regulators, including FDIC, in
the summer of 2011.

including banking institutions, investment banks, credit rating agencies, law firms, industry associations, and each of the federal banking regulators. We also reviewed data on the recent default and dividend deferral activity of trust preferred securities provided to us by a major credit rating agency.

Effects of Excluding Tier 1 Hybrid Instruments on Capital Adequacy and International Competitiveness

To assess the effects of excluding Tier 1 hybrid capital on the capital adequacy of financial institutions, we analyzed regulatory capital data to determine the extent to which bank holding companies may fall below minimum regulatory capital levels without Tier 1 hybrid instruments. We used year-end 2010 data from the FR Y-9C regulatory filing discussed previously as a baseline to compare institutions' Tier 1 capital levels before and after the hybrid capital exclusion. We assessed potential reductions in institutions' capital categories based on the Tier 1 risk-based capital ratio and Tier 1 leverage ratio. For the risk-based capital and leverage ratios, we used the capital adequacy category of well capitalized based on the levels that FDIC has identified for depository institutions under prompt corrective action standards. For the minimum capital levels for these ratios, we used benchmarks based on the Federal Reserve's bank holding company capital adequacy regulations. To consider the most significant potential effects, our analysis removed all Tier 1 hybrid instruments from all bank holding companies' Tier 1 capital. In reality, any effects will be mitigated by grandfathering, exemptions, and phase-in periods. We also collected information from interviews with regulators and industry participants and observers on the potential effects of the hybrid capital exclusion on the safety and soundness of banking institutions.

To evaluate the potential implications for international competitiveness of restricting Tier 1 hybrid capital, we reviewed studies and other documentary evidence and compared international rules on hybrid capital proposed by the Basel Committee on Banking Supervision with U.S. regulatory policy, including the Dodd-Frank Act. We also reviewed proposed rules to implement the new Basel Committee standards in Europe and reports by the Committee of European Banking Supervisors on the use of hybrid capital in Europe. We interviewed regulators, industry participants and observers, and European regulatory organizations to gather information on the effects of the hybrid capital exclusion on the international competitiveness of U.S. institutions.

For information on our analysis of the hybrid capital exclusion's potential effects on the cost and availability of credit, see appendix II.

Smaller Banking Institution Access to Regulatory Capital

To address our third objective, we conducted a nationally representative web-based survey of executives of banks, thrifts, and bank and thrift holding companies with less than $10 billion in total assets. Based on information on banking institutions provided by FDIC, OTS, and the Federal Reserve, we identified 6,733 institutions with less than $10 billion in total assets that would serve as the population for this survey. This population included all stand-alone banks and thrifts (banks and thrifts that do not have a holding company), as well as all top-level consolidated bank and thrift holding companies. We included top-level holding companies in our population rather than the subsidiary banks or thrifts because industry participants and regulators said that the holding company typically raised capital for its subsidiaries. We selected a stratified random sample of 794 institutions from the population of 6,733. We divided the population into four strata based on the amount of assets and the entity's status—that is, whether it was part of a holding company or a stand-alone bank or thrift. We designed the sample size to produce a proportion estimate within each stratum that would achieve a precision of plus or minus 7 percentage points or less at the 95-percent confidence level. We then inflated the sample size for an expected response rate of 50 percent. Because of the small number of banks and holding companies with assets greater than $5 billion and less than $10 billion, we selected all of these with certainty.

We received valid responses from 510 (64 percent) of the 794 sampled banking institutions. The weighted response rate, which accounts for the differential sampling fractions within strata, is 66 percent. We identified eight banking institutions in our sample that were either closed or were improperly included in the sampling frame. We classified these as out-of-scope institutions and adjusted our estimates so that they were generalized only to the 6,659 (+/- 58) institutions estimated to be in-scope institutions in the population.

Table 7: Population, Sample Size, and Respondent Information for GAO Survey

Stratum	Population size	Sample size	Out of scope	Respondents within scope
1. Holding company $5 billion-$10 billion	63	63	2	30
2. Holding company less than $5 billion	5,118	378	5	249
3. Banks $5 billion-$10 billion	5	5	0	4
4. Banks less than $5 billion	1,547	348	1	219
Total	6,733	794	8	502

Source: GAO survey of smaller banking institutions.

We analyzed our survey results to identify potential sources of nonresponse bias using two methods. First, we examined the response propensity of the sampled banking institutions by several demographic characteristics, including asset size, type of institution, region, regulator, and ownership status. Second, we compared weighted estimates from respondents and nonrespondents to known population values for four measures that were related to the survey outcomes we were most interested in. We conducted statistical tests of differences, at the 95-percent confidence level, between estimates and known population values, and between respondents and nonrespondents. We determined that weighting adjustments within strata would be sufficient to mitigate any potential nonresponse bias. We did not observe any significant differences between weighted estimates and known population values or between respondents and nonrespondents.

The web-based survey was administered from June 15, 2011 to August 15, 2011. We sent banking institution executives an e-mail invitation to complete the survey on a GAO web server using a unique username and password. Nonrespondents received several reminder e-mails and a letter from GAO asking them to complete the survey. The practical difficulties of conducting any survey may introduce additional nonsampling errors, such as difficulties interpreting a particular question, which can introduce unwanted variability into the survey results. We took steps to minimize nonsampling errors by pretesting the questionnaire with four banks in April 2011. We conducted pretests to make sure that the questions were clear and unbiased and that the questionnaire did not place an undue burden on respondents. An independent reviewer within GAO also reviewed a draft of the questionnaire prior to its administration. We made appropriate revisions to the content and format of the questionnaire after the pretests and independent review. All data analysis

programs were independently verified for accuracy. See appendix III for
responses to survey questions. We also collected information on
supervisory examination ratings from the Federal Reserve and FDIC to
supplement information from our survey.

To identify trends in the amount and types of regulatory capital raised by
smaller banking institutions since 2000, we analyzed data on capital
issuances. We obtained data from SNL Financial, which collects capital
issuance data from Securities and Exchange Commission filings and press
releases. We limited our review to the issuance of instruments that may be
counted as Tier 1 or Tier 2 regulatory capital by an institution's primary
federal regulator. These included common equity, preferred stock, trust
preferred securities, and subordinated debt. We discussed the data with SNL
Financial representatives to confirm our understanding of what the data
represented and what types of capital issuances were not included. The data
included offerings on public and private exchanges but did not reflect capital
raises that were not publicly offered, such as equity investments in small
institutions made by board members or local communities. Comprehensive
data on the raising of private capital were unavailable.

We also interviewed market participants, including banking institutions,
investment banks, industry associations, and federal banking regulators,
to collect information on how smaller banking institutions access
regulatory capital and challenges they face in raising capital.

For parts of our methodology that involved the analysis of computer-
processed data, we assessed the reliability of these data and determined
that they were sufficiently reliable for our purposes. Specifically, we
conducted reliability assessments on the SNL Financial data and on data
from OTS's Thrift Financial Reports. To assess the reliability of these data,
we reviewed factors such as the timeliness, accuracy, and completeness.
We conducted electronic testing and manual review to identify missing and
out-of-range data and other anomalies and compared computer-generated
data to source documents for a selected sample of companies.

We conducted this performance audit from December 2010 to January
2012 in accordance with generally accepted government auditing
standards. Those standards require that we plan and perform the audit to
obtain sufficient, appropriate evidence to provide a reasonable basis for
our findings and conclusions based on our audit objectives. We believe
that the evidence obtained provides a reasonable basis for our findings
and conclusions based on our audit objectives.

Appendix II: GAO Analysis of the Economic Effects of the Hybrid Capital Exclusion

To assess the effects on banking institutions and the economy of prohibiting the use of hybrid instruments to meet Tier 1 capital requirements, we analyzed the potential impact of this change on the cost and availability of credit. Specifically, we designed a modified version of an established econometric model to estimate the effect of a change in Tier 1 capital levels on key credit market variables, including loan volume growth and lending spreads. We also used a modified version of an existing loan pricing model to assess the impact on loan rates of banking institutions' inability to include newly issued hybrid securities as Tier 1 capital.

Vector Autoregression Model

To estimate the effect of changes to banking institutions' capital ratios on the cost and availability of credit, we estimated a modified version of a vector autoregression (VAR) model commonly used in macroeconomic and monetary research. Our VAR model consists of eight variables, including variables that serve as a proxy for the banking sector. We conducted analysis known as "innovation accounting" to trace a temporary shock to bank capital through the banking system. These techniques allowed us to form estimates of the impact of changes in capital ratios on loan growth, loan spreads, and lending standards. Our model closely follows similar analysis by Berrospide and Edge (2010), Lown and Morgan (2006), and Bernanke and Gertler (1997). We found that a negative 1 percentage point decrease in the capital ratio results in a 1.2 percentage point decline in loan volume growth and a 0.16 percentage point (16 basis points) increase in loan spreads. We calibrated these estimates to the capital shock resulting from the hybrid capital exclusion, assuming that banks have a particular capital target.

The VAR methodology provides a systematic method to capture dynamics in multiple time series and provide empirical evidence on the response of macroeconomic variables to various exogenous changes (called shocks or impulses within the framework). In contrast to structural models, VARs do not rely on detailed ex ante modeling of the relationships among the variables of interest. So long as they are present in the data during the period over which the model is estimated, many of the factors that need to be modeled separately by other estimation approaches—including international spillovers, impacts of competition or market power, and the stabilizing role of monetary policy—are incorporated implicitly.

The VAR methodology advanced by Sims (1980) treats all variables symmetrically and as potentially endogenous. That is, each variable in the model is treated as if it is influenced by other variables in the system. No structure is imposed on the variables in the model, and instead any existing causal relations are determined purely by the data itself. Each variable is expressed as a linear function of its own past values and the past values of all other variables included in the system. The equations are estimated by ordinary least squares (OLS) with the error terms representing surprise/unexpected movements in the variables after taking past values into account.[1]

The VAR methodology can be transformed to examine the dynamic reaction of each of the endogenous variables to shocks to the system.[2] This technique is often referred to as innovation accounting and involves the construction of impulse response functions. Impulse responses trace the effects of shocks or innovations to one variable through the system and examine their impacts on the other included variables. In tracing out the response of current and future values of each of the variables to a shock in the current value of one of the VAR errors, we assume that this error returns to zero in subsequent periods and that all other errors are equal to zero. Consequently, the shock is designed to be temporary. To exploit the innovation accounting framework and identify the impulse response function, we must impose some structure on the model that takes the form of simplifying restrictions. These restrictions result in causal priority given to some variables over others and are generally driven by theory. As a result, although the system incorporates feedback between all of the variables, some variables are expected to impact on others without contemporaneous feedback. As we discuss later, the ordering of variables is critically important and can impact the results in material ways.

Our VAR model consists of eight variables. The core variables that represent the macroeconomy are (1) real gross domestic product (GDP) growth, (2) GDP price inflation, (3) federal funds rate, and (4) commodity price index growth. As Lown and Morgan (2006) discuss, these four variables potentially make up a complete economy with output, price, demand, and supply all represented. We captured the banking sector with

---

[1]For more on the VAR methodology, see C.A Sims. "Macroeconomics and Reality," *Econometica*, vol. 48 (1980), 1-48.

[2]The residuals obtained from each of the estimated OLS regressions in the VAR system are combinations of underlying structural innovations.

four variables: (1) real loan volume growth—commercial bank and thrift loan growth in our base models, (2) changes in lending spreads—commercial and industrial loan rate relative to a benchmark, (3) lending standards as measured by the net fraction of loan officers at commercial banks reporting a tightening of credit standards for commercial and industrial loans (C&I) in the Federal Reserve's Senior Loan Officer Opinion Survey, and (4) the aggregate capital-to-assets ratio for the commercial banking sector. The addition of the latter four variables allows us to investigate the dynamic interaction between banks and the macroeconomy. We assembled the data from Thomson Reuters Datastream and the Federal Reserve System (table 8). We have relied on this data in our past reports and neither Thomson Reuters Datastream nor the Federal Reserve has changed their methods for collecting or reporting data since we relied on it last. We consider this data to be reliable for our purposes.

Table 8: Data Used in VAR Model

Variable	Source
Real gross domestic product (GDP)	Thomson Reuters Datastream
GDP price inflation	Thomson Reuters Datastream
Federal funds rate	Thomson Reuters Datastream
Spot commodity price index	Thomson Reuters Datastream
Lending spreads	Board of Governors of the Federal Reserve System
Real loan volumes	
Total commercial bank loans	Board of Governors of the Federal Reserve System
Total savings institution loans	Board of Governors of the Federal Reserve System
Capital-to-assets ratio (commercial bank sector)	Federal Reserve Bank of St. Louis
Lending standards	Thomson Reuters Datastream

Source: GAO.

We transformed all of the variables into growth rates except for the capital ratio and lending standards in our base models. We adjusted loan volumes for inflation as suggested by the Basel Committee on Banking Supervision's Macroeconomic Assessment Group. Using the estimated VAR system for the third quarter of 1990 through the fourth quarter of 2010, we traced out the dynamic responses of loan volumes, lending spreads, and other macroeconomic variables to shocks to the bank capital ratio. As a result, we can obtain quantitative estimates of how bank "innovations" or "shocks" affect the cost and availability of credit.

To model the relationship as validly as possible, we

- transformed the variables to ensure that they were stationary,

- selected the appropriate lag length using a formal test,

- tested formally for the stability of the system,

- determined a reasonable ordering of the variables, and

- conducted sensitivity tests.

Our base results rely on impulse response functions using the following causal ordering of the variables: GDP, GDP deflator (inflation), federal funds rate, commodity spot prices, loan volumes, capital ratio, loan spreads, and lending standards. However, we also obtained impulse response functions using an alternative ordering that gave causal priority to the banking sector variables. Although these are two extremely different ordering schemes, we found that the results were only mildly sensitive to the decision to give causal priority to the macroeconomic variables. For example, using the standard ordering of the variables, we found a 1 percentage point increase in the capital ratio yields peak effects on loan volumes and lending spreads of 0.96 percentage points and 14 basis points, while the alternative order produced peak effects of 1.4 percentage points and 17 basis points, respectively. Nevertheless, our base estimates use the average of the outcomes for the two different orderings of the variables: (1) where the macro variables are given causal priority and (2) where the bank variables are given causal priority.

We also varied the functional form in some sensitivity tests, including changing the time period analyzed and using different proxies for loan volumes and bank capital. In some sensitivity tests, we excluded the effects of the global financial crisis by running the model on the time period from the third quarter of 1990 to the third quarter of 2008. The estimated parameters from these estimates generally resulted in smaller effects on loans but larger effects on loan spreads. One finding in the literature is that C&I loans are more sensitive to changes in capital. As a result, we looked directly at the response of C&I loans to a capital shock. Our results were consistent with the literature, and we found an impact of capital changes on C&I loan volumes of about twice the size as the impact for aggregate loans. Specifically, for C&I loans, we found that a negative 1 percentage point increase in the capital ratio results in a 2.4 percentage point decline in loan volume growth and a 21 basis point increase in loan spreads.

The VAR methodology, while containing some advantages over other modeling techniques, has particular limitations, and therefore results using this approach should be interpreted with caution. First, the methodology potentially overstates the quantitative effects of shocks on the economy and can be difficult to interpret. Second, the results are heavily influenced by market and macroeconomic conditions in place during past periods of large changes in the modeled variables, so they may not be informative if similar shifts take place under different circumstances. Also, because the statistical relationships are estimated from aggregate historical data, the model may not be fully informative about how economic actors will respond to future policy changes. Third, the model parameters are aggregate estimates and may not generalize to the specific circumstances of some banks. Fourth, causal priority is given to some variables over others in order to conduct meaningful assessments of the impacts of shocks to the system. Our results, however, are not particularly sensitive to this ordering, although we do obtain larger impacts of bank capital on lending activity with some alternative orderings. To minimize this limitation, our estimates are an average of a model where causal priority is given to the macroeconomic variables and a model where causal priority is given to the bank variables. It should also be noted that VAR shocks reflect omitted variables. If the omitted variables (factors or information) correlate with included variables, then the estimates will contain omitted variable bias. Lastly, in our particular case, the impulse response functions have wide confidence intervals, suggesting considerable uncertainty in the results. Despite these limitations, the VAR approach is considered to be a reasonable alternative to other types of models. Users of the report should be aware that the VAR methodology represents one approach to analyzing the effect of bank capital on lending activity. As a result, we believe the results should be analyzed in the context of the wider body of literature on the issue. Table 9 identifies studies that we used to compare our results for reliability and consistency.

Table 9: Relevant Studies on the Impact of Capital on Lending Activity

Bank for International Settlements, "Basel III: Long-term impact on economic performance and fluctuations," BIS working paper, No. 338, Monetary and Economic Department (2011).
Bank for International Settlements, "Assessing the macroeconomic impact of the transition to stronger capital and liquidity requirements," interim report, Macroeconomic Assessment Group (August 2010).
B. Bernanke and C. Lown, "The Credit Crunch," Brookings Papers on Economic Activity 2: 205–47 (1991).
J. M. Berrospide and R. M. Edge, "The Effects of Bank Capital on Lending: What Do We Know? And What Does It Mean?," Finance and Economics Discussion Series No. 44 (Washington, D.C.: Federal Reserve Board, 2010).
Mark A. Carlson, H. Shan, and M. Warusawitharana, "Capital Ratios and Bank Lending: A Matched Bank Approach," Federal Reserve Board working paper No. 2011-34 (July 1, 2011).
T. Cosimano and D. Hakura, "Bank Behavior in Response to Basel III: A Cross-Country Analysis," IMF working paper, WP/11/119, International Monetary Fund (2011).
Douglas J. Elliott, "A Further Exploration of Bank Capital Requirements," Brookings briefing paper (Washington, D.C.: Brookings Institution, 2010).
Douglas J. Elliott, "Quantifying the Effects on Lending of Increased Capital Requirements," Brookings briefing paper (Washington, D.C.: Brookings Institution, 2009).
M. King, "Mapping Capital and Liquidity Requirements to Bank Lending Spreads," BIS working paper, No 324, Bank of International Settlements (2010).
C. Lown and D. Morgan, "The Credit Cycle and the Business Cycle: New Findings Using the Loan Officer Opinion Survey," Journal of Money, Credit, and Banking 38 (6): 1575–97 (2006).
Jan Vlcek and S. Roger, "Macroeconomic Costs of Higher Bank Capital and Liquidity Requirements," IMF working paper 11/103, International Monetary Fund (2011).
P. Slov k and B. Cournede, "Macroeconomic Impact of Basel III," OECD Economics Department Working Papers, No. 844, (Paris: Organization for Economic Cooperation and Development Publishing, 2011).

Source: GAO.

Loan Pricing Model

To assess the impact of the inability of banking institutions with greater than $500 million in assets to include newly issued hybrid securities as Tier 1 capital, we utilized a modified version of a loan pricing model following Elliott (2009, 2010). This methodology is designed to illustrate that banking institutions have multiple options for adjusting to more costly forms of Tier 1 capital and allows us to consider these different scenarios and show the implied change in lending rates. Given the variety of ways that banks can adjust and the degree of competition in loan markets, we found that the impact on lending rates will likely be modest.

Our framework is a simple mathematical model that is based on a loan pricing equation where the price of the loan is such that it must at least cover the weighted cost of capital, expected credit losses, and administrative expenses. We augment the equation found in Elliott (2009, 2010) by decomposing equity into common equity and equitylike instruments (hybrid capital) that qualify as Tier 1 capital. Assuming that the loan is priced so that the rate charged at least covers the weighted cost of capital and that institutions hold common equity and hybrid capital as equity, we can write the following:

$$L*(1-t) >= (E*(EK*r_{ce} + EH*r_{tps}(1-t))+((D*r_d)+C+A-O)*(1-t)$$

Where:

L = effective interest rate on the loan

t = marginal tax rate for the bank

E = proportion of equity backing the loan

r_{tps} = required rate of return (yield) on the marginal hybrid securities (trust preferred securities)

r_{ce} = required rate of return (yield) on the marginal common equity

EK = proportion of equity held as common equity

EH = proportion of equity held as hybrid securities (trust preferred securities)

D = Proportion of debt and deposits funding the loan

r_d = Effective marginal interest rate on D

C = the credit spread (equal to probability weighted expected loss on the loan portfolio)

A = administrative and other expenses related to the loan

O = other offsetting benefits to the bank of making the loan

This formula is used to capture the lower cost of hybrid securities, including the associated tax benefits (EH*rtps(1-t)). In practice these instruments are largely trust preferred securities. As a result, we use the yield on trust preferred securities as our proxy for the yield on the class of hybrid instruments. We assume that the yield on hybrid capital is 8.65 percent based on our review of a small sample of actual trust preferred securities. For smaller banking institutions, we increase the yield on hybrid capital slightly to 9 percent. For the aggregate banking sector, we assume that institutions hold 12 percent of their Tier 1 equity in the form of hybrid securities based on our analysis of banking data from SNL Financial. Similarly, based on our analysis, we assume that smaller institutions hold a larger percentage of hybrid securities as equity—19 percent. We initiated our model using the assumptions laid out in Elliott (2009, 2010) but then made modest adjustments to calibrate the loan rate to the actual yield on loans for the commercial banking sector (5.6 percent). For smaller banking institutions, we used Elliott's (2010) assumptions for banks with $1 billion to 10 billion in assets with minor modifications. For example, we assumed that smaller institutions had a higher probability-weighted loss on loan portfolios. The remaining assumptions not discussed here are contained in table 6.

Our scenario analysis is designed to illustrate how the loan rate might be affected given various assumptions about banking institutions' responses and other mitigating factors. However, because there is limited empirical foundation for many of our initial values, the assumptions underlying the analysis and estimates for the loan rate should not be considered definitive. Our analysis is designed to illustrate how the cost of credit might change given various assumptions about institutions' responses and other factors, rather than arrive at precise estimates for the level of loan rates. Moreover, because we focused our analysis on the aggregate banking sector, the actual impact on and response by individual institutions can differ depending on a number of dynamics. For example, we have assumed that banking institutions have the ability to pass on higher costs to borrowers in the form of higher lending rates, to some degree. However, some institutions may have to resort to asset sales, thereby reducing the total amount of their risk-weighed assets or undertaking other actions due to the inability to pass on the higher cost of capital to customers.

Appendix III: Responses to Questions from GAO's Survey of Smaller Banking Institutions

We sampled 794 stand-alone banks and thrifts (those with no holding company) and top-level bank holding companies and thrift holding companies with total assets of less than $10 billion from the population of 6,733 to examine the options these smaller institutions have for raising capital. We received valid responses from 510 (64 percent) out of the 794 sampled institutions. Tables 10-24 show the responses to questions from the survey. Because we followed a probability procedure based on random selections, our sample is only one of a large number of samples that we might have drawn. Since each sample could have provided different estimates, we also provide the lower and upper bound estimates at a 95 percent confidence interval. The weighted response rate, which accounts for the differential sampling fractions within strata, is 66 percent. For more information about our methodology for designing and distributing the survey, see appendix I.

Table 10: How Likely Is It That Your Institution Would Be Able to Raise the Following Types of Regulatory Capital at Acceptable Cost, Terms, and Conditions within the Next Year?

Responses		Estimated percentage	95 percent confidence interval— lower bound (percentage)	95 percent confidence interval— upper bound (percentage)
Equity investments from board members or local community	Very likely	32	28	37
	Somewhat likely	38	33	43
	Not likely	23	19	27
	No basis to judge	6	4	9
Common equity from public offering	Very likely	8	5	11
	Somewhat likely	19	16	23
	Not likely	57	52	61
	No basis to judge	16	13	20
Common equity from private placement	Very likely	12	9	16
	Somewhat likely	34	29	38
	Not likely	39	34	44
	No basis to judge	15	12	18
Preferred equity from public offering	Very likely	4	3	7
	Somewhat likely	13	10	17
	Not likely	60	55	64
	No basis to judge	23	19	27

Responses		Estimated percentage	95 percent confidence interval— lower bound (percentage)	95 percent confidence interval— upper bound (percentage)
Preferred equity from private placement	Very likely	6	4	9
	Somewhat likely	24	20	28
	Not likely	48	43	53
	No basis to judge	22	18	26
Trust preferred securities	Very likely	2	1	4
	Somewhat likely	10	7	13
	Not likely	66	62	71
	No basis to judge	22	18	26
Subordinated debt	Very likely	6	4	9
	Somewhat likely	23	19	27
	Not likely	51	46	56
	No basis to judge	20	16	23
Other	Very likely	4	2	8
	Somewhat likely	4	2	8
	Not likely	31	25	38
	No basis to judge	61	54	67

Source: GAO survey of smaller banking institutions from June 15, 2011, to August 15, 2011.

Note: Examples of "Other" responses included the U.S. Treasury Department's Small Business Lending Fund and mutual institutions that raise capital exclusively through profits.

Table 11: How Important Are Each of the Following Factors in Determining Your Institution's Ability to Successfully Raise Capital?

Responses		Estimated percentage	95 percent confidence interval— lower bound (percentage)	95 percent confidence interval— upper bound (percentage)
Financial condition and performance (e.g., profitability, debt and capital levels, asset quality)	Very important	87	83	90
	Somewhat important	9	7	12
	Not important	1	0	2
	No basis to judge	3	2	5
Growth potential	Very important	49	44	54
	Somewhat important	41	37	46
	Not important	6	4	9

Responses		Estimated percentage	95 percent confidence interval— lower bound (percentage)	95 percent confidence interval— upper bound (percentage)
	No basis to judge	4	2	6
Management quality	Very important	74	70	78
	Somewhat important	19	15	23
	Not important	2	1	4
	No basis to judge	4	3	6
Size of institutions/offering	Very important	28	24	33
	Somewhat important	51	47	56
	Not important	12	9	16
	No basis to judge	8	6	11
Liquidity of capital instrument	Very important	30	26	35
	Somewhat important	51	46	56
	Not important	11	8	15
	No basis to judge	7	5	10
Economic environment in lending area	Very important	47	42	52
	Somewhat important	45	40	50
	Not important	4	2	6
	No basis to judge	5	3	7
Capital market conditions	Very important	39	34	44
	Somewhat important	43	38	48
	Not important	10	7	13
	No basis to judge	8	6	11
Familiarity with investors	Very important	45	40	50
	Somewhat important	39	34	44
	Not important	7	5	10
	No basis to judge	9	7	12

Responses		Estimated percentage	95 percent confidence interval— lower bound (percentage)	95 percent confidence interval— upper bound (percentage)
Ability to conduct public offerings	Very important	18	14	21
	Somewhat important	27	22	31
	Not important	33	28	37
	No basis to judge	23	19	27
Other	Very important	6	3	11
	Somewhat important	4	2	9
	Not important	14	9	21
	No basis to judge	75	68	82

Source: GAO survey of smaller banking institutions from June 15, 2011, to August 15, 2011.

Note: Examples of "Other" responses included the regulatory environment and structure as a mutual institution.

Table 12: If Your Institution Had to Replace 10 Percent of Its Tier 1 Capital *Within 2 Years*, How Likely Is It That It Would Do Each of the Following?

Responses		Estimated percentage	95 percent confidence interval— lower bound (percentage)	95 percent confidence interval— upper bound (percentage)
Issue new equity	Very likely	32	27	36
	Somewhat likely	34	29	39
	Not likely	29	25	34
	No basis to judge	5	3	7
Reduce dividend payments	Very likely	39	34	43
	Somewhat likely	16	13	20
	Not likely	29	25	34
	No basis to judge	15	13	18
Increase operating efficiency, including by reducing compensation or other costs	Very likely	38	33	43
	Somewhat likely	44	40	49
	Not likely	16	13	20
	No basis to judge	1	0	3

Responses		Estimated percentage	95 percent confidence interval— lower bound (percentage)	95 percent confidence interval— upper bound (percentage)
Raise average margins between borrowing and lending rates	Very likely	26	21	30
	Somewhat likely	48	43	53
	Not likely	26	22	30
	No basis to judge	1	0	2
Increase non-interest income	Very likely	22	18	26
	Somewhat likely	49	44	54
	Not likely	28	23	32
	No basis to judge	1	0	2
Lower the size of loan portfolios	Very likely	18	14	21
	Somewhat likely	36	31	40
	Not likely	46	41	51
	No basis to judge	1	0	2
Reduce or sell non-loan assets	Very likely	13	10	17
	Somewhat likely	32	28	37
	Not likely	51	46	56
	No basis to judge	3	2	5
Shift balance sheet composition toward less risky assets	Very likely	15	12	19
	Somewhat likely	48	43	53
	Not likely	33	28	37
	No basis to judge	4	2	6
Other	Very likely	6	3	12
	Somewhat likely	3	1	8
	Not likely	13	7	20
	No basis to judge	78	70	85

Source: GAO survey of smaller banking institutions from June 15, 2011, to August 15, 2011.

Note: Examples of "Other" responses included retain earnings and increase borrowing.

Table 13: If Your Institution Had to Replace 10 Percent of Its Tier 1 Capital *Within 5 Years*, How Likely Is It That It Would Do Each of the Following?

Responses		Estimated percentage	95 percent confidence interval—lower bound (percentage)	95 percent confidence interval—upper bound (percentage)
Issue new equity	Very likely	31	26	35
	Somewhat likely	34	30	39
	Not likely	32	27	36
	No basis to judge	4	2	6
Reduce dividend payments	Very likely	29	25	34
	Somewhat likely	21	17	25
	Not likely	36	31	40
	No basis to judge	14	11	16
Increase operating efficiency, including by reducing compensation or other costs	Very likely	34	30	39
	Somewhat likely	47	42	52
	Not likely	17	14	21
	No basis to judge	1	0	3
Raise average margins between borrowing and lending rates	Very likely	30	26	34
	Somewhat likely	45	40	50
	Not likely	24	20	28
	No basis to judge	1	0	2
Increase non-interest income	Very likely	26	22	30
	Somewhat likely	51	46	56
	Not likely	22	18	26
	No basis to judge	1	0	2
Lower the size of loan portfolios	Very likely	10	7	13
	Somewhat likely	34	29	38
	Not likely	55	50	60
	No basis to judge	1	0	2
Reduce or sell non-loan assets	Very likely	10	7	13
	Somewhat likely	36	31	41
	Not likely	52	47	57
	No basis to judge	2	1	4

Responses		Estimated percentage	95 percent confidence interval—lower bound (percentage)	95 percent confidence interval—upper bound (percentage)
Shift balance sheet composition towards less risky assets	Very likely	12	9	15
	Somewhat likely	49	44	54
	Not likely	36	31	40
	No basis to judge	4	2	6
Other	Very likely	7	3	14
	Somewhat likely	4	1	9
	Not likely	15	9	23
	No basis to judge	73	64	81

Source: GAO survey of smaller banking institutions from June 15, 2011, to August 15, 2011.

Note: Examples of "Other" responses included retain earnings and increase borrowing.

Table 14: Has Your Institution Raised Regulatory Capital Since January 1, 2008?

Responses	Estimated percentage	95 percent confidence interval—lower bound (percentage)	95 percent confidence interval—upper bound (percentage)
Yes	35	31	40
No	65	60	69

Source: GAO survey of smaller banking institutions from June 15, 2011, to August 15, 2011.

Table 15: During Which of the Following Time Periods Did Your Institution Raise Capital? For the Time Period, Consider the Date of Offering or Issuance.

Responses		Estimated percentage	95 percent confidence interval—lower bound (percentage)	95 percent confidence interval—upper bound (percentage)
January 1, 2011—present	Raised capital	35	27	43
	Did not raise capital	65	57	73
January 1, 2010—December 31, 2010	Raised capital	50	41	59
	Did not raise capital	50	41	59
January 1, 2009—December 31, 2009	Raised capital	54	45	63
	Did not raise capital	46	37	55
January 1, 2008—December 31, 2008	Raised capital	39	30	47
	Did not raise capital	61	53	70

Source: GAO survey of smaller banking institutions from June 15, 2011, to August 15, 2011.

Note: Results reflect the responses of those that answered "Yes" to the question "Has your institution raised regulatory capital since January 1, 2008?"

Table 16: Did the Amount of Regulatory Capital Your Institution Raised Meet Its Target/Goal?

Responses	Estimated percentage	95 percent confidence interval— lower bound (percentage)	95 percent confidence interval— upper bound (percentage)
Yes	82	74	88
No	18	12	26

Source: GAO survey of smaller banking institutions from June 15, 2011, to August 15, 2011.

Note: Results reflect the responses of those that answered "Yes" to the question "Has your institution raised regulatory capital since January 1, 2008?"

Table 17: Did the Regulatory Capital Your Institution Raised Meet Its Initial Terms and Conditions?

Responses	Estimated percentage	95 percent confidence interval— lower bound (percentage)	95 percent confidence interval— upper bound (percentage)
Yes	93	87	96
No	7	4	13

Source: GAO survey of smaller banking institutions from June 15, 2011, to August 15, 2011.

Note: Results reflect the responses of those that answered "Yes" to the question "Has your institution raised regulatory capital since January 1, 2008?"

Table 18: What Types of Regulatory Capital Has Your Institution Raised Since January 1, 2008?

Responses		Estimated percentage	95 percent confidence interval—lower bound (percentage)	95 percent confidence interval—upper bound (percentage)
Equity instruments from board members or local community	Raised capital	58	50	67
	Did not raise capital	42	33	50
Common equity from public offering	Raised capital	11	6	17
	Did not raise capital	89	83	94
Common equity from private offering	Raised capital	29	22	37
	Did not raise capital	71	63	78
Preferred equity from public offering	Raised capital	1	0	5
	Did not raise capital	99	95	100
Preferred equity from private offering	Raised capital	5	2	10
	Did not raise capital	95	90	98
Trust preferred securities	Raised capital	4	1	8
	Did not raise capital	97	92	99
Subordinated debt	Raised capital	14	8	22
	Did not raise capital	86	78	92

Responses		Estimated percentage	95 percent confidence interval—lower bound (percentage)	95 percent confidence interval—upper bound (percentage)
Federal government capital programs (such as the Capital Purchase Program and Community Development Capital Initiative)	Raised capital	28	21	36
	Did not raise capital	72	64	79
Other	Raised capital	25	15	36
	Did not raise capital	75	64	85

Source: GAO survey of smaller banking institutions from June 15, 2011, to August 15, 2011.

Note: Results reflect the responses of those that answered "Yes" to the question "Has your institution raised regulatory capital since January 1, 2008?" Examples of "Other" responses included operating income and the exercise of stock options.

Table 19: What Were the Reasons Your Institution Did Not Raise Regulatory Capital Since January 1, 2008?

Responses		Estimated percentage	95 percent confidence interval—lower bound (percentage)	95 percent confidence interval—upper bound (percentage)
No need for or interest in raising additional regulatory capital?	A reason	88	84	92
	Not a reason	12	8	16
Lack of capital raising options (for reasons including: unfavorable market conditions, lack of investor interest, etc.)	A reason	20	15	26
	Not a reason	80	74	85
Tried to raise capital but was unable to do so	A reason	3	1	6
	Not a reason	97	94	99
Other	A reason	18	10	27
	Not a reason	82	73	90

Source: GAO survey of smaller banking institutions from June 15, 2011, to August 15, 2011.

Note: Results reflect the responses of those that answered "No" to the question "Has your institution raised regulatory capital since January 1, 2008?" Examples of "Other" responses included institutions that are already well capitalized and mutual institutions that are not allowed to raise capital except through retained earnings.

Table 20: In Your Opinion, How Challenging, If at All, Is the Current Regulatory Capital-Raising Environment for Your Institution?

Responses	Estimated percentage	95 percent confidence interval—lower bound (percentage)	95 percent confidence interval—upper bound (percentage)
Very challenging	44	39	49
Moderately challenging	32	28	37
Not challenging	12	9	16
No opinion	11	9	15

Source: GAO survey of smaller banking institutions from June 15, 2011, to August 15, 2011.

Table 21: How Challenging, If at All, Are Each of the Following Factors in Your Institution's Ability to Raise Regulatory Capital?

Responses		Estimated percentage	95 percent confidence interval—lower bound (percentage)	95 percent confidence interval—upper bound (percentage)
Lack of rating by credit rating agency	Very challenging	6	4	9
	Moderately challenging	20	16	24
	Not challenging	31	26	35
	No opinion / not applicable	43	38	48
Lack of equity analyst coverage	Very challenging	8	5	11
	Moderately challenging	17	13	21
	Not challenging	31	26	35
	No opinion / not applicable	44	40	49
Lack of access to public capital markets	Very challenging	16	12	20
	Moderately challenging	25	20	29
	Not challenging	22	18	26
	No opinion / not applicable	38	33	42
Investor preference for larger offering size	Very challenging	16	13	20
	Moderately challenging	19	15	23
	Not challenging	27	23	31
	No opinion / not applicable	38	33	42
Transaction costs of conducting a public offering (including underwriting costs)	Very challenging	22	18	26
	Moderately challenging	26	22	30
	Not challenging	19	15	23

Responses		Estimated percentage	95 percent confidence interval—lower bound (percentage)	95 percent confidence interval—upper bound (percentage)
	No opinion / not applicable	34	29	38
Economic climate and/or market conditions	Very challenging	46	41	51
	Moderately challenging	28	24	33
	Not challenging	9	7	13
	No opinion / not applicable	16	13	19
Investor perception of your institution's financial condition (for example, based on factors including amount of debt or non-performing assets)	Very challenging	19	15	23
	Moderately challenging	25	21	29
	Not challenging	37	32	41
	No opinion / not applicable	19	16	23
Composition of your institution's existing capital structure (for example, existence of trust preferred securities)	Very challenging	5	3	8
	Moderately challenging	15	12	19
	Not challenging	48	44	53
	No opinion / not applicable	31	27	35
Laws and regulations	Very challenging	33	28	38
	Moderately challenging	36	31	40
	Not challenging	11	8	15
	No opinion / not applicable	20	16	24

Source: GAO survey of smaller banking institutions from June 15, 2011, to August 15, 2011.

Table 22: How Does the Current Ability of Your Institution to Raise Regulatory Capital Compare to the Ability to Raise Regulatory Capital Prior to the Recent Financial Crisis (Consider the Time Period before 2008)?

Responses	Estimated percentage	95 percent confidence interval—lower bound (percentage)	95 percent confidence interval—upper bound (percentage)
Much more difficult than before	41	36	45
Somewhat more difficult than before	26	21	30
Equally as easy or difficult as before	10	7	13
Somewhat easier than before	1	0	2
Much easier than before	0	0	2
Uncertain	7	5	10
No opinion	15	12	19

Source: GAO survey of smaller banking institutions from June 15, 2011, to August 15, 2011.

Table 23: Prior to January 1, 2008, How Beneficial, If at All, to Your Institution's Access to Regulatory Capital Was Its Ability to Issue Trust Preferred Securities (Including Pools of Trust Preferred Securities)?

Responses	Estimated percentage	95 percent confidence interval—lower bound (percentage)	95 percent confidence interval—upper bound (percentage)
Greatly beneficial	20	16	24
Moderately beneficial	9	7	13
Not at all beneficial	10	7	13
No opinion	10	7	13
Not applicable: my institution did not issue any trust preferred securities.	50	46	55

Source: GAO survey of smaller banking institutions from June 15, 2011, to August 15, 2011.

Table 24: In Your View, How Will the Following Recent and Proposed Changes to Regulatory Capital Requirements Affect Your Institution's Ability to Raise Regulatory Capital, If at All?

Responses		Estimated percentage	95 percent confidence interval—lower bound (percentage)	95 percent confidence interval—upper bound (percentage)
The Dodd-Frank Act's prohibition on hybrid capital instruments, such as trust preferred securities, from consideration as Tier 1 regulatory capital	Greatly decrease	24	20	29
	Somewhat decrease	17	14	21
	No change	29	24	33
	Somewhat increase	4	3	7
	Greatly increase	3	1	5
	No opinion	23	19	27
Basel III (changes to the definition of capital (including Tier 1 capital), changes to the calculation of risk-weighted assets, and changes to capital ratio requirements)	Greatly decrease	18	15	22
	Somewhat decrease	22	18	26
	No change	21	17	25
	Somewhat increase	7	5	11
	Greatly increase	3	2	5
	No opinion	28	24	32

Source: GAO survey of smaller banking institutions from June 15, 2011, to August 15, 2011.

Appendix IV: GAO Contact and Staff Acknowledgments

GAO Contact	Thomas J. McCool, (202) 512-2642 or mccoolt@gao.gov
Staff Acknowledgments	In addition to the contact named above, Daniel Garcia-Diaz (Acting Director), James Ashley, Kevin Averyt, Emily Chalmers, William R. Chatlos, Rachel DeMarcus, M'Baye Diagne, Lawrance Evans Jr., Richard Krashevski, Jill Lacey, Courtney LaFountain, Marc Molino, Patricia Moye, Michael Pahr, and Maria Soriano made key contributions to this report.

GAO's Mission	The Government Accountability Office, the audit, evaluation, and investigative arm of Congress, exists to support Congress in meeting its constitutional responsibilities and to help improve the performance and accountability of the federal government for the American people. GAO examines the use of public funds; evaluates federal programs and policies; and provides analyses, recommendations, and other assistance to help Congress make informed oversight, policy, and funding decisions. GAO's commitment to good government is reflected in its core values of accountability, integrity, and reliability.
Obtaining Copies of GAO Reports and Testimony	The fastest and easiest way to obtain copies of GAO documents at no cost is through GAO's website (www.gao.gov). Each weekday afternoon, GAO posts on its website newly released reports, testimony, and correspondence. To have GAO e-mail you a list of newly posted products, go to www.gao.gov and select "E-mail Updates."
Order by Phone	The price of each GAO publication reflects GAO's actual cost of production and distribution and depends on the number of pages in the publication and whether the publication is printed in color or black and white. Pricing and ordering information is posted on GAO's website, http://www.gao.gov/ordering.htm. Place orders by calling (202) 512-6000, toll free (866) 801-7077, or TDD (202) 512-2537. Orders may be paid for using American Express, Discover Card, MasterCard, Visa, check, or money order. Call for additional information.
Connect with GAO	Connect with GAO on Facebook, Flickr, Twitter, and YouTube. Subscribe to our RSS Feeds or E-mail Updates. Listen to our Podcasts. Visit GAO on the web at www.gao.gov.
To Report Fraud, Waste, and Abuse in Federal Programs	Contact: Website: www.gao.gov/fraudnet/fraudnet.htm E-mail: fraudnet@gao.gov Automated answering system: (800) 424-5454 or (202) 512-7470
Congressional Relations	Katherine Siggerud, Managing Director, siggerudk@gao.gov, (202) 512-4400 U.S. Government Accountability Office, 441 G Street NW, Room 7125 Washington, DC 20548
Public Affairs	Chuck Young, Managing Director, youngc1@gao.gov, (202) 512-4800 U.S. Government Accountability Office, 441 G Street NW, Room 7149 Washington, DC 20548